Northern
Chihuahuan Desert

Wildflowers

A FIELD GUIDE TO
WILDFLOWERS AND OTHER PLANTS
OF THE DESERT AND ITS PARKLANDS

By Steve West
Carlsbad Caverns–Guadalupe Mountains Association

FALCON®
HELENA, MONTANA

Published in cooperation with **the Carlsbad Caverns–Guadalupe Mountains Association.**

A FALCON GUIDE®

Falcon® is continually expanding its list of recreational guidebooks. All books include detailed descriptions, accurate maps, and all the information necessary for enjoyable trips. You can order extra copies of this book and get information and prices for other Falcon® guidebooks by writing Falcon®, P.O. Box 1718, Helena, MT 59624 or calling toll-free 1-800-582-2665. Please ask for a free copy of our current catalog. Visit our website at www.Falcon.com or contact us by e-mail at falcon@falcon.com.

1 2 3 4 5 6 7 8 9 0 RG 05 04 03 02 01 00

Falcon and FalconGuide are registered trademarks of Falcon Publishing, Inc.

Editing: Rose Houck, Rick LoBello
Project Coordination: Rick LoBello, Gayle Shirley
Design, typesetting, and printing: Falcon Publishing, Inc.
Illustrations by DD Dowden

Library of Congress Cataloging-in-Publication Data

West, Steve, 1949-
    Chihuahuan Desert Wildflowers : a field guide to commom wildflowers, shrubs, and trees
/ by Steve West.
        p. cm.
    Includes bibliographical references (p.).
    ISBN 1-56044-980-2 (pbk.)
      1. Wild flowers--Chihuahuan Desert--Identification. 2. Shrubs--Chihuahuan Desert--Identification. 3. Trees--Chihuahuan Desert--Identification. 4. Wild flowers--Chihuahuan Desert--Pictorial Works. 5. Shrubs--Chihuahuan Desert--Pictorial works. 6. Trees--Chihuahuan Desert--Pictorial works. I. Title.
QK 142.2 . W47 2000
581.754'09764'9--dc21
                                                                                00-025835

CAUTION

All participants in the recreational activities suggested by this book must assume responsibility for their own actions and safety. The information contained in this guidebook cannot replace sound judgment and good decision-making skills, which help reduce risk exposure; nor does the scope of this book allow for disclosure of all the potential hazards and risks involved in such activities.

Learn as much as possible about the recreational activities in which you participate, prepare for the unexpected, and be cautious. The reward will be a safer and more enjoyable experience.

CONTENTS

Dedicated to all those who struggle for environmental justice; for the sake of our children, they must succeed. To my daughters and grandchildren; they have taught me to appreciate that each day is a wondrous opportunity to learn. And to the clammyweed, buffalo gourd, stinkbugs, centipedes, vinegaroons, vultures, and skunks; we share this incredible journey with them.

Acknowledgments

No book is written without the help, encouragement, and assistance of many people. The idea for this book was first suggested by Bob Peters, and without him, the first of many, many steps would not have been taken. Many people who served on the board of the Carlsbad Caverns–Guadalupe Mountains Association assisted, most notably Larry Coalson and Doug Lynn, Jr. Their backing of the idea for this book was critical, always positive and always helpful. Rick LoBello was instrumental in making this book a reality; his enthusiasm, good spirit, and concern was vital in seeing this project through. At times when the goal seemed out of reach, he showed me it was still possible. He made valuable suggestions throughout, and his professionalism and dedication to the CCGMA is evident in all that he does.

Special thanks to Fred Armstrong, Bill Dunmire, Bill Route, Barton Warnock, and Rick Spellenberg for their help in reviewing the manuscript.

I thank my parents, who gave me the luxury as a kid to explore the desert. A deep debt is also owed to John Phillips, a brother in spirit who explored the desert with me during our teen years. My thanks also go to friends who offered words of encouragement and company while exploring the Chihuahuan Desert and so many other natural places: Tom Bemis, Bobby Click, Craig Cranston, Mike Medrano, Wallace Merchant, Frank Smith, Brent Wauer, Tom Wootten, and Jack West. And to the far too many others to be named, I apologize.

Two individuals need to be singled out. The first is Ron Egan, one of the most decent people anyone could have the honor of knowing. The second is Tommy Joe Hines, knowledgeable about the desert and always enthusiastic about learning. He is a great companion of good humor who will never finish asking questions. And that is what life should be about.

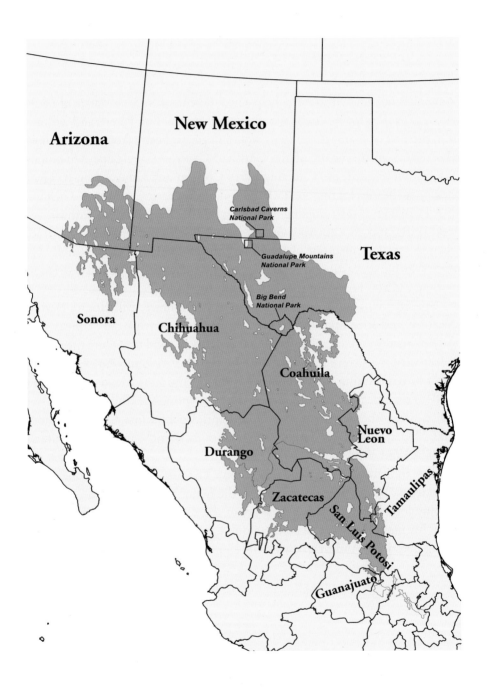

The Chihuahuan Desert

Source: World Wildlife Fund

$\mathscr{I}$NTRODUCTION

This guidebook to the wildflowers, shrubs, and trees of the northern Chihuahuan Desert is intended for the general public. It enables the reader to identify some of the more common as well as unusual plants found throughout the northern Chihuahuan Desert within the United States.

The Chihuahuan Desert is probably one of the least-known deserts in the country. As a biologic entity, the Chihuahuan Desert has no fixed boundaries as do states and nations. With some exceptions, the boundaries discussed here are the same as those outlined in *Deserts* (MacMahon, 1992). Note, however, that although much of the high country of the Guadalupe Mountains is an "island" in the desert, it is included here as well.

North American Deserts

Ecologists generally identify four deserts in North America: the Great Basin, Sonoran, Mojave, and Chihuahuan. Each exhibits unique plants and animals, distinctive climate, and other identifying features.

The Great Basin Desert covers a large portion of Nevada, western Utah, and a corner of Oregon. At its higher elevations, it is the coldest of the four North American deserts. The Great Basin Desert is the largest desert area wholly within the United States, occupying about 158,000 square miles (409,220 sq km).

The Sonoran Desert encompasses southern Arizona, southern California, much of Baja California, and the western coast of Mexico. The classic indicator plant of this desert is the tree-sized saguaro cactus *(Cereus giganteus)*. A large, biologically diverse desert, the Sonoran occupies about 106,000 square miles (274,540 sq km). Because of varied soils and a two-season rainfall pattern, this desert is especially rich in life forms.

Wedged between the Sonoran and Great Basin Deserts is the Mojave Desert, which includes parts of Utah, Nevada, California, and Arizona. It is the smallest of the four deserts, occupying only 54,000 square miles (139,860 sq km). The Joshua tree *(Yucca brevifolia)* is the indicator plant of the Mojave.

Covering 175,000 square miles (453,250 sq km), the Chihuahuan Desert is the largest of the four. It was not delineated until 1948, when L. R. Dice defined it as a separate biogeographic province. In the United States, the

Chihuahuan Desert occurs primarily in southern New Mexico and Texas, with a small portion in southeastern Arizona. More than 70 percent of this desert is in Mexico.

Overall, the Chihuahuan Desert is colder and mostly wetter than the Sonoran. It has an extremely rich flora. Although no list is complete, the U.S. portion of the Chihuahuan Desert alone would include at least 1,500 species of plants. The indicator plant is the lechuguilla *(Agave lechuguilla)*.

Climate, topography, soil types, and distribution of plants and animals are all used to define a particular desert, but biological boundaries are not subject to strict delineation. Transition zones between desert and nondesert areas are often extensive and change over time.

The primary shapers of the Chihuahuan Desert are its inland location, the tropical influence from the south, and the "rain shadow" effect of surrounding mountains. As warm, moist air is forced upwards when it encounters a mountain, it cools and releases its moisture, causing lands to be dry on the other side. Elevation ranges within the Chihuahuan Desert are extreme—the lowest point occurs along the Rio Grande on the United States–Mexico border at about 820' (250 m), with a high point of 6562' (2000 m). Average elevation is about 4593' (1400 m).

Precipitation varies widely throughout the Chihuahuan Desert from year to year. As a general rule, rainfall ranges from less than 8" (20 cm) to almost 20" (50 cm). Although most moisture arrives as rain in the summer, it can come year-round in lesser amounts. Occasional local storms deliver great amounts of moisture and produce flooding. Minimal moisture results from snowfall.

Relative humidity is low, usually between 40 and 60 percent. Around impoundments and along rivers, though, relative humidity can be quite high, having a long-term effect on nearby plant communities. Construction of numerous dams along the Rio Grande, Pecos, and other rivers has in many instances provided wetter habitats for plants. Consequently, the character of plant communities has changed, at least locally.

Winds can be severe, with greatest velocities from February through May. High winds, however, are possible nearly anytime. Wind has always been an important agent in dispersing seed and pollen. Wind and dust devils, for example, have probably played a role in dispersing the seeds of plants endemic to isolated gypsum areas.

Four of the eight different physiographic provinces noted for the Chihuahuan Desert are found within the area covered in this book: Great Plains, Gulf Coastal Lowland, Northern Sierra Madre Oriental, and Basin and Range. The first three, though limited in size, provide much of the biodiversity in this desert. The Great Plains Province, in the northeast, occurs totally within the United States; the average elevation is 2461' (750 m). Including much of the Pecos River basin south to the foothills of the Davis Mountains, it acts as a transition zone into the shortgrass areas to the north and east.

The Gulf Coastal Lowland Province begins as an alluvial plain that extends gradually to the east from Big Bend National Park along the Rio Grande floodplain. This province is a transition between the Chihuahuan Desert, the Edwards Plateau of west-central Texas, and the tropical region of southern Texas and northeastern Mexico.

The Northern Sierra Madre Oriental Province includes the high portions of the Davis and Chisos Mountains in western Texas. These mountains are mostly volcanic in origin, with striking escarpments and irregular profiles. Their plant communities exhibit a strong Mexican influence.

The Basin and Range Province, largest of all, includes large sections of the U.S. share of the Chihuahuan Desert. It is characterized by north-south trending mountains separated by large basins or valleys filled with the eroded material from the nearby mountains. Many of the mountain ranges contain peaks in excess of 6500' (2000 m). While largely dry now, the Basin and Range Province contains evidence of old drainage patterns indicating periods of much more water in the past.

Another way to describe the Chihuahuan Desert is by defining the plant communities. Medellin-Leal (in Bender, 1982) described four primary plant community types. The largest is the Microphyllous Desertic Brushwood Community, which is the "typical" Chihuahuan Desert habitat (and most other North American deserts as well). It occurs up to the highest elevations in the Chihuahuan Desert and accounts for nearly half the area treated in this book.

Plants of this community have small leaves that produce a wide variety of resins. In growth form, most are shrubby or subshrubby; many possess thorns. Creosotebush and tarbush are among the most representative of these plants, and in some places these two are almost all that is found. *Acacia* and *Ephedra* may also be abundant. The most common cacti are *Opuntias* (both pad and cholla type), but many other cacti occur with less frequency. In other areas yucca and mesquite are common, with mesquite often dominant.

This small-leaved shrub and tree community has been used extensively for agriculture and livestock grazing. Although the land is potentially productive, irrigated soils are susceptible to salt accumulation. Irrigation has also lowered water tables; this and salinization have lead to significant changes in this plant community. Mesquite, for example, has increased greatly because of grazing trends in the Southwest.

The second community, Desert Grassland, likely originated from specific physical and chemical characteristics of the soil. The boundaries of this community are difficult to determine because grazing has altered much of the historic grassland. These areas have been invaded by species from nearby regions that are toxic or unpalatable to cattle—including snakeweed, acacia, creosotebush, *Opuntia* cactus, mesquite, yucca, and many others. These plants that cattle will not eat often increase in disturbed areas, giving a false picture of what should be a historic plant community.

The Sclerophyllous Brushwood Community is generally limited in this part of the Chihuahuan Desert to elevations greater than 3281' (1000 m). The increasing relative humidity is the determining factor for here rather than rock and soil types. This community sees heavy human use, and continued disturbance over time has led to increasing overall aridity.

Finally, the Aciculifolious-Squamifolious Low Forest Community is extremely limited here, being mostly in Mexico; it represents another step toward more humid conditions. It is found at higher elevations and includes trees such as pine and juniper. This community is generally open. Like the brushwood community, it is also susceptible to disturbance.

The origin of Chihuahuan Desert plants is still not totally clear. A look at the big picture shows that the varied communities arose from many sources at different times. The first colonizers probably came from the tropics and included species from the genera *Acacia, Cassia, Mimosa, Solanum,* and others. Endemics probably developed with invasions of this area as it was uplifted. Uplifting and similar geologic activity resulted in geographic barriers, which enhanced speciation. The number of endemic forms in the Chihuahuan Desert, those found here and nowhere else, is relatively high compared with other North American deserts.

Next to arrive were species adapted for low water use. These established themselves on rocky slopes where they faced less competition. Neotropical elements later colonized volcanic areas.

The presence of species such as pine and aspen, which are now generally limited to higher, cooler elevations, evinces a time when the climate was cooled by glaciers farther north and in the highest mountains.

Changes Since European Arrival

Plant communities constantly change. Environmental influences mold them, form new species, and cause others to die out. Determining what they were like a hundred, a thousand, or ten thousand years ago is difficult. Fortunately, we now have a variety of tools to give us clues.

Looking at current plant populations can provide some information about past communities and illustrate how striking some changes have been. For example, the presence of quaking aspen in the higher parts of the Guadalupe, Davis, and Chisos Mountains indicates that sometime in the past, the climate here was likely cooler. Likewise, cooler, moister north-facing slopes in these dry mountains harbor plants now known primarily from the north.

Examination of pollen from thousands of years ago has also given ideas of previous plant communities (Martin, 1963). Even studying the contents of preserved dung of extinct animals such as the Shasta ground sloth provides good information about what grew here when these animals roamed the region (Spaulding and Martin, 1979).

While this region has been getting continuously warmer and drier for some time, the last century has brought more change. For eons bison periodically visited this part of the Chihuahuan Desert, and they and the grasslands evolved together. When bison were removed and cattle introduced, plant communities began to change drastically. Bison would move through an area, consume much of the forage, and then move on. Cattle, though, are often kept in one area without giving the land a chance to rest. The result has been destruction, and even effective elimination, of grassland communities. Topsoil is lost, springs and creeks silt in or dry up, riparian areas are destroyed, and former grassland is covered with impenetrable scrub and other plants cattle will not eat. The botanical change leads to changes in the animals that depend on the plants. In critical riparian areas, some species have been extirpated.

Many land managers now rotate stock, allowing the land and its vegetation to rejuvenate, with some encouraging results. But the results of past detrimental actions are still apparent in national parks in the Southwest as well as on other lands.

National Park Areas

The focus of the book is on plants found within eight National Park Service areas in the region: Carlsbad Caverns, Guadalupe Mountains, Big Bend, White Sands, and the Rio Grande Wild and Scenic River. Also included are Amistad National Recreation Area, Chamizal National Memorial, and Fort Davis National Historic Site. In these significant natural areas, enthusiasts have the best opportunity to see many of the species profiled here. The plants in this book can also be found in areas adjoining the parks, including the Lincoln National Forest of New Mexico.

Amistad National Recreation Area

Amistad National Recreation Area features three different biological environments. Elements of the Edwards Plateau hill country and of the brush country typical of southern Texas and Tamaulipas in northeastern Mexico occur there, along with Chihuahuan Desert elements. The Chihuahuan Desert influence is especially strong in the western portion of the recreation area.

Amistad Dam began storing water on May 31, 1968, permanently altering the plant and animal communities along the Rio Grande and surrounding areas. Fragments of these historic communities are much more limited now and occur where water levels have not altered the environment.

Amistad is best known for fishing and boating, but it also offers much for hikers and naturalists. Stop at the visitor center north of Del Rio for an orientation and suggestions of good places to hike and see flowers blooming. Note that the canyons hold plant communities different from the surrounding, relatively dry tablelands.

Big Bend National Park

Big Bend National Park is the largest park covered in this book, totaling 1251 square miles (3242 sq km). With such a large natural area, this park is a "must-

RICK LOBELLO

Lower elevations of Big Bend National Park.

see" for anyone who wants to begin to appreciate the natural communities of the northern Chihuahuan Desert.

More than one thousand species of plants have been recorded within the boundaries of Big Bend National Park. This high number reflects the park's size and the varied habitats within its boundaries.

The lowest elevation in the park, on the east side of the Rio Grande, is 1722' (525 m). About 35 miles (48 km) to the southwest is the highest point, Emory Peak, at 7835' (2388 m). Many other high points in the Chisos Mountains provide a wide view of much of the park. At these elevations, you are often surrounded by oak and pine, which are more typical of the Sierra Madre of Mexico, while you also gain an expansive look at lowland Chihuahuan Desert communities.

Plant communities in Big Bend National Park have changed since European arrival. Early European visitors made little comment about the state of the grasslands, but there is good evidence that healthy communities existed throughout the Big Bend area. In 1860, W. H. Echols reported abundant grass and timber at Castolon, although neither can be reported as abundant there today. Grass was "stirrup high" in the Terlingua Valley, a description distinctly wrong today. Tobosa grass hay was harvested from Tornillo Creek and Tobosa Flat near Mariscal Mountain in the early 1900s (Maxwell, 1985). That too is no longer the case. These examples show, however, that even as recently as 1900, some grassland communities in the Big Bend were in good shape. But in the former days of open range, humans rarely cast an eye to the future. Often land was stocked to the maximum levels.

Drought followed in the 1910s and that, coupled with continuous grazing by cattle, horses, goats, and other livestock, without adequate rest of the range, depleted the once-rich communities. Stock were moved to higher ground in surrounding mountains, and soon those areas were overgrazed as well. While grasslands were allowed to partly recover for short periods, they shrank as their time for recovery diminished.

When Big Bend became a national park, people who owned the future park lands began selling their private holdings to the government in 1941 and 1942. But they were allowed free grazing rights, which did not expire until January 1, 1945. This resulted in one final, heavy stocking of the range, which further depleted limited forage, increased growth of brush, and accelerated soil erosion, which had already become severe.

Compounding the problems was the very dry year of 1944. Though stock counts were rarely accurate, an estimated forty thousand cows, goats, sheep, and horses were in Big Bend during the summer of 1944. This number is far above what the land could normally sustain, especially during a drought.

Recovery since 1945 has been slow, and in some areas almost nonexistent, though reseeding projects, begun in 1947, have occasionally produced encouraging local results. Probably because of higher rainfall, mountain slopes have recovered more rapidly than, for instance, lower-elevation washes. Observers will find some lowland areas gradually recovering, but they will also still see abundant lechuguilla and shrubs. Unfortunately, it will take many more years before anyone will see large expanses of "stirrup high" grass across much of the lowland areas of the park, if it ever happens. Topsoil removal during periods of overgrazing will limit the amount of recovery anticipated even under the best conditions.

Wauer (1971) divided the park into five ecological zones, from river floodplain to the moist Chisos woodland areas. Though the zones overlap, distinct communities can be discerned. The **river floodplain–arroyo** community (less than 1 percent of the park) occurs in lowland areas of the park along the Rio Grande and its tributaries, many of which are ephemeral.

This community is found from about 1804' (550 m) to 4000' (1220 m) elevation. Because of the periodic flooding to which they are subjected, plants of this community are fast growing, broadleaf, and thicket producing. Common plants include cottonwood, willow, and cane. They can be seen at most places along the river, but the best example is at Rio Grande Village, especially along the nature trail.

The **shrub desert** occurs from about 1804' (550 m) to as high as 3500' (1067 m). Almost 49 percent of the park falls within this category. This is what most visitors call the "desert." Characteristically it has low rainfall and widely spaced shrubs, with many succulents and thorn bushes.

Above the shrub desert begins the **sotol grassland** community. This and the shrub desert are the two major plant communities; the sotol grassland occupies another 49 percent of the park. Greater rainfall here supports grasslands with tall shrubs. The community extends from 3200' (975 m) to 5500' (1676 m).

The fourth community is the **woodland,** from 3700' (1127 m) to 7800' (2377 m), restricted to only about 2 percent of the park. This community is characterized by broadleaf trees and, in the Chisos Mountains, conifers.

The last plant community is the **moist Chisos woodland,** covering less

RICK LOBELLO

Grasslands in Big Bend National Park were overgrazed in the early 1900s and have yet to recover.

than 1 percent of the area, composed of Arizona cypress, bigtooth maple, several species of oaks, and even an isolated population of quaking aspen. It is very small, occupying only about 800 acres (324 ha). This forest-edge habitat is found only in localized areas in Boot and Pine Canyons and along the northeastern slopes of the East Rim. It occurs from about 5000' (1524 m) to 7200' (2194 m) in elevation.

Big Bend National Park is a gem of the National Park system. With wide vistas and rich biodiversity, it is a park where you can spend a great deal of time. It is worth seeing at different seasons; be sure to take a hike on some of the backcountry trails or drive on the lesser-traveled roads. Though Big Bend is somewhat isolated, once you are there, it is a difficult place to leave.

Carlsbad Caverns National Park

Carlsbad Cave National Monument, in southeastern New Mexico, was set aside on October 25, 1923, in a proclamation signed by President Calvin Coolidge. The protected surface area was not large, and the park was greatly expanded on May 14, 1930, when President Herbert Hoover signed a bill establishing Carlsbad Caverns National Park. Final boundary adjustments were completed in 1963 and included the addition of Rattlesnake Springs to the park. Carlsbad Caverns National Park now contains 73 square miles (189 sq km).

Elevations within the park range from 3596' (1096 m) at Rattlesnake Springs to 6386' (1946 m) in the western portion. The plant list for Carlsbad Caverns includes over seven hundred species. Almost all of Carlsbad Caverns National Park consists of dry limestone escarpments and canyon bottoms covered with stands of sotol, lechuguilla, yucca, prickly pear, Mexican orange, Mexican buckeye, and various grasses. A few trees can be found, including Texas madrone, western soapberry, and netleaf hackberry. Higher elevations along the western edge support thick stands of juniper and scattered ponderosa pine.

The canyon bottoms and springs nurture different plant communities. Species that require more moisture are found here, along with thicker stands of Texas madrone and other trees including ponderosa pine and bigtooth maple. Chinkapin oak, known only locally at Carlsbad Caverns, can be found near the scattered springs in the area.

Visitors can see the various plant communities at several select spots. One

RICK LOBELLO

Lower elevations of Carlsbad Caverns National Park.

is Walnut Canyon, along the park entrance road from Whites City to the visitor center. Short trails head off from several pullouts along the road, and signs along the trails describe the plants.

A nature trail leaves from the park visitor center, follows the escarpment for a short distance, goes down into Bat Cave Draw, then ends up back at the visitor center. The 9-mile (15-km) Walnut Canyon Desert Drive west of the visitor center winds along the top of the escarpment, drops into the canyon, and rejoins the Walnut Canyon Road near the base of Big Hill.

One can also walk any of several backcountry trails. Along with beautiful scenery, these hikes offer many opportunities for botanical discoveries. Slaughter Canyon and Yucca Canyon provide easily accessible, moderate hikes.

Rattlesnake Springs, though small, hosts a wide variety of plants different from those found in the rest of the park. Most of the western part of Rattlesnake Springs exhibits a typical lowland plant community of acacia, mesquite, littleleaf sumac, allthorn, and honey mesquite. The springs itself and Rattlesnake Creek are an example of an endangered ecosystem in the southwestern deserts. Such riparian areas have been greatly altered over the past two hundred years. While this one too has changed, many original elements remain, including willows,

RICK LOBELLO

The Rattlesnake Springs area of Carlsbad Caverns National Park.

cottonwoods, hemlocks, cattails, and sedges. Even a solitary Mexican elder, *(Sambucus mexicana),* the only one known in the park, grows here. Most of the creek bed on the southern side of the park is owned by The Nature Conservancy. A trail follows the fence line, giving a good view of the creek and the flourishing plant and bird life.

Chamizal National Memorial

Chamizal National Memorial is located amid the largest twin cities on the United States–Republic of Mexico border: El Paso, Texas, and Ciudad Juarez, Chihuahua. The memorial was designated to commemorate the permanent establishment of the international boundary between the United States and Mexico and the continuing friendship between the two nations. The Republic of Mexico has established a similar park on its side of the Rio Grande that is well worth a visit.

A few native species have been planted at Chamizal, but very little of the original plant community remains. El Paso and Juarez occupy large portions of the river bottom, and native plant communities are long gone. Only near Las Cruces, New Mexico, can remnants of these original riparian communities still be found, but even there they are greatly altered.

Levees now confine the Rio Grande in a human-made channel, but in isolated spots there are still some stands of native plants. Beyond Las Cruces, in the stretch between Radium Springs and Hatch, there are better examples of these communities, but introduced saltcedar has taken over large areas of the floodplain. Mesquite, willow, cottonwood, and wolfberry occur, along with many others.

Fort Davis National Historic Site

Fort Davis National Historic Site was originally established in 1963. This small Park Service site is located within the limits of Fort Davis, Texas. Preserved there is a fort that figured prominently in the settlement of west Texas, protecting settlers on their way west.

The park occupies 0.72 square mile (1.9 sq km). Much of the site consists of historic buildings and offers little "natural" habitat. Still, more than 250 species of plants in 64 families are known to occur in the park.

The park brochure includes a map of trails visitors can walk to see wildflowers to the north and west of the restored areas. One of the best is the Tall Grass Nature Trail, which continues on to the North Ridge Trail and eventually to Davis Mountains State Park. In all these areas, the timing and amount of rain will heavily influence what you find. One spring or early fall may be fantastic while the one the following year may be disappointing.

The general area of Fort Davis has an interesting plant community including good stands of cottonwood along Limpia Creek. Other worthwhile destinations nearby include Davis Mountains State Park to the west and Lake Balmorhea to the north.

Guadalupe Mountains National Park

On October 13, 1966, the U.S. Congress established Guadalupe Mountains National Park, and in 1972 the park was dedicated. This added a second national park to the state of Texas, and it is one of the hidden treasures of the park system.

The park currently includes 135 square miles (349 sq km). Some of the low-lying gypsum and quartz sandhills on the western boundary were added to the park in 1998. Sixty percent of the park has officially been designated as wilderness, which should help protect this area in its natural state for generations to come.

El Capitan Peak in Guadalupe Mountains National Park.

The highest point in Texas occurs in this park. Guadalupe Peak, at 8749' (2667 m), is a commanding presence in all directions.

The plant life at Guadalupe Mountains National Park has been well studied compared to many other sites in the Chihuahuan Desert. An annotated checklist prepared in 1981, along with later studies, have resulted in approximately nine hundred species of plants recorded in the park.

Several authors have delineated four to five vegetative zones for Guadalupe Mountains. First is **desert,** which includes most of the park land on the western, eastern, and southern escarpments. Most areas in the park below 5000' (1524 m) fit this category, with some as high as 6500' (1981 m). Dominant species include those found throughout the lowland Chihuahuan Desert covered by this book—creosotebush, honey mesquite, lechuguilla, viscid acacia, tarbush, and four-wing saltbush. Grasses do not generally make up a major component of this community although this may be a result of past grazing practices. The extent of historic grassland is not clear, but at present the community is better classified as desert scrub rather than as grassland.

Above the desert scrub, and in regions that gradually receive more moisture and less evaporation, are the **woodland** communities. Many of the previously mentioned desert species occur here but in lower densities. Some of the species common in the woodland communities are New Mexico agave, sotol, little walnut, gray oak, chinkapin oak, Knowlton hop-hornbeam, and Texas madrone.

The **McKittrick Canyon** area contains a woodland community with a rich variety of plants with extremely limited distributions in the region. At higher elevations, one-seed juniper and two-needle pinyon appear in increasing numbers.

The **forest** zone is very restricted, found only at the highest elevations such as at the Bowl, in the upper reaches of McKittrick Canyon, and similar sites. The large conifers, ponderosa pine and Douglas-fir, make up this community. A small population of quaking aspen even grows on the western edge of the Bowl.

Plants associated with **rock outcrops,** though they do not fit well with any of the other communities, include a number of rare and interesting species at widely separated sites in the park, including both east- and west-facing escarpments, Dog Canyon, and McKittrick Canyon. Some of the many species associated with rock outcrops are cliff fendlerbush, Hitchcock mockorange, button cactus, and McKittrick pennyroyal.

To get a good grasp of the park's plant communities, a visitor should sample a variety of sites. Hikes up McKittrick Canyon and to the Bowl should be considered a minimum for a good introduction. Roads lead to the lowland areas, including Dog Canyon, and other low places. Guadalupe Mountains National Park has many botanical wonders; even a short visit will enrich one's life.

Rio Grande Wild and Scenic River

Rio Grande Wild and Scenic River, established in 1978, encompasses a little more than 200 miles (323 km) of the Rio Grande. The western end is at the middle of Mariscal Canyon and the wild-and-scenic portion ends south of Dryden, Texas. Most visitation consists of float trips traveling downriver. The plants here are somewhat typical of those subjected to periodic flooding. The community is similar to those in Big Bend National Park to the west, where the plants are much easier to view.

White Sands National Monument

White Sands National Monument is located 15 miles (24 km) southwest of Alamogordo, New Mexico. On the northern edge of the Chihuahuan Desert, White Sands is a unique area that protects a large portion of the world's largest collection of gypsum dunes. Preserved along with the glistening white dunes are unusual plant and animal communities that have evolved to survive in this specialized habitat.

White Sands was first declared a monument on January 18, 1933. The current boundaries include 144,420 acres (58,446 ha). The park's elevation averages about 4000' (1200 m). The low point occurs at South Lake Lucero at 3872' (1180 m). The high point is 4117' (1255 m). None of the park land is currently designated as wilderness, although much of it is de facto wilderness.

The White Sands plant community has many similarities to the smaller gypsum area east of Dell City, Texas, the only other significant gypsum dunes in the United States (now within Guadalupe Mountains National Park). With little change in habitat, White Sands has a relatively small flora, only about 175 species.

Five distinctly different habitats have been identified. The **alkali flat and Lake Lucero** community has very few species and a low biomass. Except for a few grasses, the predominant plant is pickle-weed. The lake bed supports few plants because on rare occasions there is too much water, and most often there is none. The highly alkaline condition of the lake bed also prevents most plants from becoming established.

Alluvial fans, or bajadas, flank the western edge of White Sands, the result of erosion from the San Andres Mountains. Only the lower areas of the alluvial fans are in the park. Washes, which occasionally fill with water, dissect the fans. Creosotebush and honey mesquite are the dominant shrubs on the fans.

The **marginal dunes,** mostly in the southern and eastern parts of the monument, are parabola-shaped dunes that are more stable compared to others. Plants that live there include hoary rosemary-mint, skunkbush sumac, and the occasional Rio Grande cottonwood. Soaptree yucca is also quite common and, like many other plants that grow in dunes, has an extensive root system to hold the plant in place, which acts to stabilize the dunes.

The **saltbush flats** currently consist mostly of four-wing saltbush, but a grassland community quite different than what is present today once occupied this area. Grasses today are sparse, and the land has not recovered from droughts and the heavy impact of relatively large numbers of grazing animals. The saltbush flats are widespread in other desert areas, particularly north of the dunes through the Tularosa Basin.

What most visitors come to White Sands to see are the high, elegant **transverse and barchan dunes.** These dunes are gradually moving; in the process, they cover plants in their path. Although some plants such as soaptree yucca and Rio Grande cottonwood occur infrequently, annuals do better in this community because of the temporary, mobile nature of the habitat.

Garton Lake, just east of park headquarters, is a small body of spring-fed surface water. Found in this specialized, local habitat are plants that can grow here, and only here, because of the presence of water. It is a friendly environment for the introduced saltcedar, but it also provides a refuge for native species such as salt-marsh bullrush, narrowleaf and common cattail, and seepwillow baccharis.

The Future

If we want to save even an echo of the former richness of these lands, we need to look to the past and to the future and try to determine how we can preserve and even restore the native Chihuahuan Desert.

Looking into the next century, we can be certain of one thing—plant communities will continue to change. As in the past, new species will originate from a variety of sources. Some will be exotic invaders, aided in their colonization by human activities. Others will naturally migrate in as the climate changes or as species adapt.

Many of these additions will be slow and gradual, others will be more rapid. Some of the abrupt changes may result in the extirpation of species that presently occur in the Chihuahuan Desert. Some species may only die out in this region, while others will become extinct globally. Some types of changes, such as long-term, natural climate variation, are to some degree out of our hands. But we are responsible for others that can have permanent, devastating effects.

If left alone, or if managed properly, national parks and similarly protected areas can serve as refuges where natural processes can continue unfettered. Many of these areas experienced dramatic ecological changes before they were established as parks. While recovery is apparent in some, others are not much better than when the park was established.

On public and private lands surrounding national parks, the ethic of protecting native communities is seldom the prevailing philosophy. Oil and gas development, mineral extraction, urban sprawl, ranching, and other activities are taking place on these lands. While some ranchers practice rest-rotation grazing, others continue the age-old practice of leaving cattle on the range without giving the land a chance to rest.

In addition, other introduced animals, such as aoudad or Barbary sheep, are unfortunately filling the role of the native mountain sheep, now extirpated from the Guadalupes. Oryx at White Sands and goats at Carlsbad Caverns have taken a toll on fragile plant communities in those parks as well. The money, resources, and political will are not often readily available to completely remove these unwelcome exotics.

Human population pressure is increasing, too. As more people move to the Southwest, parks feel their presence. These newcomers will use limited water resources, and they will want more open space. Can parks satisfy these increasing demands and retain their natural qualities, one of many reasons for which they were set aside?

The future rests in our hands. While all species, to varying degrees, shape the future of other species, *Homo sapiens* has a special ability—and responsibility—to do so. We still have time to correct past mistakes. But every lost element of the richness of life leaves us that much less flexible in our choices. By removing plants and animals from this remarkable web of life, we are stealing from our children and their children. We end up living in a poorer world. We must address these difficult problems with diligence, so that we might more accurately predict the consequences of our actions, act accordingly, and leave something of the fascinating Chihuahuan Desert for future generations.

How to Use This Guide

Anyone with an interest in the Chihuahuan Desert of western Texas and southern New Mexico can use this guide as a tool for understanding the unique tapestry of plants found in the region. The book is designed to be used without any specialized knowledge, and technical terms have been eliminated, with a few necessary exceptions. There are hundreds of species of native flowering plants in this spectacular mountain region. This guide covers the more common and characteristic plants.

Included here are photographs and descriptions of 261 plants. Plants are grouped according to three major categories: cactus and other succulents; flowers, organized by color; and trees, shrubs, and other plants. The flower color categories are **white, pink and purple, green, blue, orange and red, and yellow.** Within each category, the entries are arranged in order from more ancestral to more derived, so that monocots, such as lilies, are listed first, and dicots, such as the mustards, mints, and sunflowers, proceed in phylogenetic order toward the back. Each plant description also includes abbreviations of the National Park areas where you might find some of the plants in this book. These abbreviations are:

BBNP = Big Bend National Park
CCNP = Carlsbad Caverns National Park
FDHS = Fort Davis National Historic Site
GMNP = Guadalupe Mountains National Park
WSNM = White Sands National Monument

Flower color is a convenient means of quickly grouping plants, but it is by no means a perfect system. Wildflowers, like all living things, are variable; no two individuals are exactly alike. The variation results from a combination of heredity ("what were the parents like?") and environment ("what are the conditions where it grows?"). Just as there may be blond-, black-, and red-haired people, a single species of plant may have a range of flower colors. Many plants with pink flowers, for instance, also have white-flowered forms. Grouping plants by color also is problematic because the difference between colors, such as blue and purple, is sometimes difficult to define. Plus, some plants even have multicolored flowers. In this guide, plants are grouped according to the color that is most prevalent for the species. With this book, the best way to begin to identify a Chihuahuan Desert wildflower is to go to the color section that matches the plant in question.

The written entry accompanying each plant photograph includes both the common and scientific names of the plant. Note that most plants have several common names, and a common name used in one region may apply elsewhere to a totally unrelated plant. The common names used in this book are selected to be the most appropriate throughout the Chihuahuan Desert region. In some instances, additional common names are given in the Comments section of each entry. Scientific names, however, do not vary from region to region and are unique for each species.

We have attempted to follow the most accepted usages of scientific names. Different scientific names for the same species are often noted from text to text. This is true because interpretations of the multitude of species change as investigations continue and new information comes to light.

Two books were especially important and indispensable in this work. The *Manual of the Vascular Plants of Texas* by Correll and Johnston (1970) was the primary source of information on many Texas species. Similarly, *A Flora of New Mexico* by Martin and Hutchins (1980) was the accompanying work for that state.

The *Arizona Flora* by Kearney and Peebles was also consulted. In addition, several books on specific families or groups were useful. *Cacti of Texas and Neighboring States* by Weniger was the primary taxonomic source for the cacti, a group that can be especially confusing.

Common names can only add to the confusion. For some species of plants, a multitude of common names appear in the literature and even more have been used by people who live in an area and are familiar with the species. Native Americans undoubtedly had names for many of these plants, but most of them have been lost in time and with the destruction of those cultures. This is an immeasurable loss. As I interviewed specialists in the course of making this book, I learned of many additional names for plants that were not acknowledged elsewhere in print. For example, I collected at least 18 common names for the widespread cactus *Opuntia leptocaulis*. Usually the most appropriate common name was also the most widespread one, and in many cases a Spanish name appeared most appropriate and was most widespread.

Some common plant names, in use for many generations, express sexist, racist, or other biases; these names may in fact be objectionable to some people. In these cases, I attempted to find an unbiased common name to substitute. Still, occasional names may be deemed inappropriate by some people. In those instances, I apologize and hope someday our language will be rid of all names that denigrate people and their cultures. There is no reason to use the natural world to foster continued misunderstanding, ignorance, and prejudice. While this may seem a minor concern to some, it is not to others. If we cannot treat one another as equals, how can we hope to understand and appreciate other living things with which we share this planet and on which we depend so much?

Because of the confusion surrounding common names, the scientific name of the plant also is provided. These names, rendered in Latin, are a more stable and universal means of referring to a particular plant; scientific names are recognized worldwide and are unique to the organisms they identify. A scientific name consists of two words. The first word, the genus (plural genera), is the name of a group of plants with similar general characteristics. The second part of the scientific name is the specific epithet, or specific name, which identifies the particular species of plant.

Thus there are often many species within a single genus. Besides being consistent, scientific names show relationships by identifying species in the same genus. For example, *Echinocereus triglochidiatus,* the scientific name for claret-cup cactus, identifies it as the species *triglochidiatus,* part of the larger genus *Echinocereus.* A close relative is *Echinocereus chloranthus,* the green-flowered torch cactus.

Genera are grouped into families according to similarities in their structure and biology. The scientific name of a plant family always ends with the suffix *-aceae,* such as Cactaceae for the cactus family. With surprisingly little experience, many common plant families can be identified at first sight. Most people are already familiar with the unmistakable flowers of the legume family (Fabaceae), which includes peas, beans, sweet peas, lupines, and locust flowers. Being able to determine the family of an unknown plant helps in field identification.

The main part of each entry contains a description of the plant. This description starts with general growth characteristics and identifying features. Leaves, flowers, and sometimes fruits are described. For many features, such as plant height, leaf size, and flower dimensions, the typical size (or range of sizes) is given in U.S. and metric measurements. Unless otherwise stated, leaf measurements are for the leafy part of the plant only, and do not include the leaf stalk. The size ranges given are for typical plants. No size measurements are absolute, and diligent searching will reveal the odd, stunted individual or the overfertilized giant. However, the measurements provided here will apply to most of the plants encountered.

When identifying plants in the field, it helps to take a minute to study the plant, noting its general growth form, leaves, flowers, and any other distinguishing features. Look around for other plants of the same species. Maybe you will see better-developed or more fully blooming individuals. A small magnifying glass with a 10x magnification helps in seeing telltale hairs, flower parts, and other minute features.

The descriptions and photographs in this book are intended to be used together to identify a plant. There may be occasions when a plant does not exactly match an entry but clearly is a close relative. In many cases, this will be because the plant in question is of a different species but the same genus as the plant in the photograph. Sometimes, the Comments section mentions related species and how to identify them.

Although this guide keeps technical terms to a minimum, users will find knowledge of a few special terms immeasurably helpful. These terms, easy to learn and useful for all plant identification, are discussed below. A list of terms is included in the glossary at the back of this book.

Many of the plants listed in this book are perennial, that is, parts of the plant live anywhere from a few years to more than a century. Familiar examples of perennial plants include cacti, yuccas, and oak trees. Perennial plants can be divided into two types: woody plants such as trees and shrubs, and herbaceous plants that die back to ground level each year, with only the underground parts overwintering. Most Chihuahuan Desert plants are herbaceous perennials; only a small percentage are woody plants. In addition to perennials, herbaceous plants may be classified as annuals, which germinate, flower, produce seeds, and die within a year, or biennials, which take two years to produce seeds before dying.

It often is easy to recognize that a plant is perennial since parts of the previous year's growth may be visible. Perennial plants generally have well-developed underground parts such as bulbs or large tuberous roots, while annual plants typically have a small system of fibrous roots. Plants discussed in this book are perennial unless stated otherwise; also, all plants in the book are herbaceous unless they are specifically listed as woody.

Each plant description provides the diagnostic features needed for identification, including discussion of overall appearance, leaves, and flowers. Sometimes, features such as fragrant leaves or colored or milky sap will be mentioned. These can be determined by gently squeezing and then smelling a leaf, and by slightly tearing the tip of a leaf and noting the sap color. Some plants have winged parts, thin strips of tissue attached edgewise along a stem, branch, or other part.

Another feature often useful in plant identification is the presence of hairs on leaves, stems, or flower parts. Some plants are always hairless, some are always hairy, and individual plants within some species may range from hairless to hairy. Noting the size, abundance, and type of hairs is often useful for identification purposes. In this guide, the discussion for each plant includes whether the plant is hairy or smooth, if this is a useful feature for identification. If the hairiness is not mentioned, it means that the plant can be smooth or hairy; or that the hairs are small, sparse, and easily overlooked.

Leaves are important identifying features of wildflowers. To describe small differences precisely, botanists use dozens of technical terms for the shapes, textures, surfaces, margins, parts, and attachments of leaves. This book avoids such terms. Leaf shapes are described using common language such as "long and narrow" or "broadly oval."

Important leaf features to note include arrangement of the leaves on the stem (opposite each other, alternating along the stem, or whorled, with several leaves originating from one point); whether the leaves are on stalks or stalkless, and characteristics of the leaf itself, such as the leaf tip (pointed or blunt), leaf base (tapering, rounded, heart-shaped, or clasping the stem), leaf edges (smooth, toothed, wavy, or lobed), and leaf texture (thick, leathery, waxy, thin, or brittle). Many plants produce basal leaves; these leaves originate directly from the underground parts of the plant and are not attached to the stems. Sometimes, the shape of the basal leaves may differ from the stem leaves or the basal leaves may have different stalks.

Any leaves not identified as compound are simple leaves (see Figure 1A on following page). Simple leaves have a single, leaflike blade above each bud. This blade may be lobed or unlobed, but it is clearly a single leaf. Compound leaves are divided into two or more distinct segments called leaflets, with each segment often looking like a separate leaf. The only sure way to identify a compound leaf is to look for buds. If there are several leaflike segments above a single bud, you are dealing with a compound leaf. This identification can be tricky, but is important to master since many plant groups can be quickly determined by this feature. Leaflets of compound leaves can be arranged like a feather, along a stalklike axis, or they can originate from a common point like the fingers on a hand; they can even be doubly or triply compound, with each segment divided once or twice again into further series of leaflike segments. In all cases, however, the leaflets of compound leaves are arranged in the same plane.

Figure 1. Variations of Leaf Arrangement (A), Shape (B), and Margin (C)

A. Leaf Arrangement

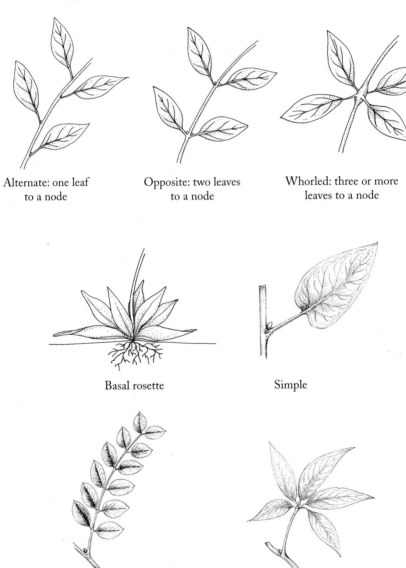

Alternate: one leaf
to a node

Opposite: two leaves
to a node

Whorled: three or more
leaves to a node

Basal rosette

Simple

Pinnately compound leaves: leaflets
arranged on both sides of the petiole

Palmately compound leaves: leaflets
spreading like fingers from the
palm of the hand

B. Leaf Shape

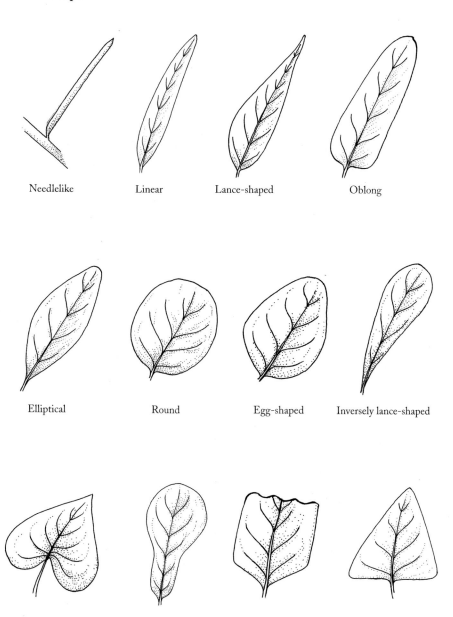

Needlelike

Linear

Lance-shaped

Oblong

Elliptical

Round

Egg-shaped

Inversely lance-shaped

Heart-shaped

Spatula-shaped

Wedge-shaped

Triangular

C. Leaf Margin

Entire   Toothed   Wavy

Lobed   Doubly toothed   Cleft

Bracts are reduced, leaflike structures or scales that are often associated with flowers. Sometimes bracts are like miniature versions of the plant's leaves. They might also appear as little pointed or rounded green scales, or be totally different in size and shape from the leaves. Bracts may be green and leaflike in texture, thin and papery, but sometimes they are colored like flower petals.

Flowers are the most complicated parts of a plant. They come in an array of shapes, sizes, and colors. Flower descriptions in this guide are intended to help in identification, so only prominent or distinctive flower characteristics are discussed. Lack of discussion of a particular feature does not mean it is lacking for that species, but only that it is not a useful characteristic for identification.

Flowers have one main function: to facilitate pollination of the female flower parts, which develop into seeds and fruits. Flowers that are insect pollinated often have showy or fragrant parts to attract suitable pollinators. On the other hand, flowers that are wind pollinated, such as many trees and grasses, have very reduced flowers suited to launching and capturing wind-blown pollen without the need for showy or fragrant parts.

A diagram of a generalized flower is given in Figure 2. Most flowers have an outer series of flower parts, called sepals, surrounding the base of the flower. Sepals often are green and can be inconspicuous, but they also can be showy and colored. The sepals together form the calyx. The calyx may be composed of separate sepals, or the sepals may be joined or fused into a tube or cuplike calyx. If the sepals are fused, they often are represented by teeth or points around the top of the calyx.

Inside the calyx of most flowers is a series of usually showy parts called petals. These are what we first see when we view the average flower. The petals come in a variety of shapes, sizes, and colors, and, depending on the kind of plant, there may be no petals or three to six or more per flower. The petals may be separate from each other or partially or wholly fused together into a cuplike, tubular, or irregular shape. The petals together, whether fused or separate, form the corolla. Some flowers have no corolla and in some plants, the sepals and petals are identical and are called tepals.

Within the flower, pollen is produced by the stamens. There may be one to more than a hundred stamens per flower. Stamens typically are long, thin filaments with clublike or elongate appendages at the tip. The seed-producing part of the flower is called the pistil. This consists of the usually swollen ovary

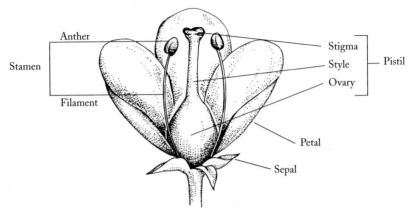

Figure 2 . Typical flower in cross section

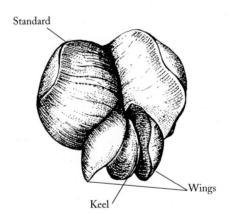

Figure 3. Flower of the Bean Family (Fabaceae)

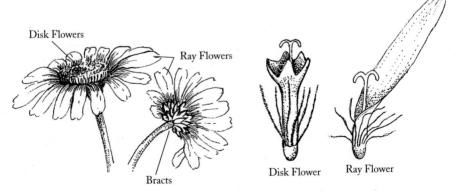

Figure 4. Flowers of the Sunflower Family (Asteraceae)

where the seeds develop, above which is a usually long, tubelike style with a blunt, divided, or elongate stigma at the tip that serves as a pollen receptor. In some flowers, the style is absent. While most flowers have both male (stamen) and female (pistil) parts, some plants have separate male and female flowers and in some species, male and female flowers are on separate plants.

The arrangement of flowers on a plant also is useful for identification purposes. Again, botanists use many specialized terms to describe the arrangement of flowers on a plant. Because these terms could be confusing to a general readership, they are kept to a minimum here. Flower arrangements are generally described in terms such as "open clusters" or "narrow elongate spikes."

Two families of flowers, both well represented in the Chihuahuan Desert, have specialized flower structures that deserve comment. Most plants in the legume family (Fabaceae) have a calyx surrounding five petals that are developed into a specialized form. The upper petal, called the standard, is erect, spreading, and usually the largest. Below this are two protruding side petals, called wings, closely surrounding the keel, which is actually formed by the fusion of the two lowest petals. A typical legume family flower is shown in Figure 3.

Asters, goldenrods, sunflowers, dandelions, and other plants in the sunflower family (Asteraceae) have an unusual flower arrangement. What appears at first glance to be a single flower is actually a head composed of a few to several hundred small flowers. This head of flowers usually is surrounded at the base by a series of bracts. The calyx on each little flower is absent or reduced to bristles, scales, or hairs. Two kinds of flowers are produced: disk flowers and ray flowers (Figure 4), as described below.

The corollas of ray flowers are lengthened on one side into a single, usually brightly colored strap that looks like the petal of a conventional flower. Disk flowers have small, tubular corollas, usually with five lobes. Depending on the species, each flower head may be all disk flowers, all ray flowers, or a combination of the two. When both are present, there usually is a central circle or cone of disk flowers surrounded by one or more series of ray flowers, the whole creating the appearance of a single typical flower, even though there may be more than a hundred flowers present. A typical sunflower family flower head is diagrammed in Figure 4.

Following the **Description** of each plant is a section titled **Habitat/Range.** This provides a summary of the typical Chihuahuan Desert habitats for the plant and a general range where the plant grows within the region. These habitat statements apply only to the northern Chihuahuan Desert in the United States.

The **Habitat/Range** section also includes comments about the relative abundance of plants, using terms such as *common, limited,* and *rare.* These are general terms to give the user an idea of the relative rarity of each species, but they are intended merely as rangewide guides. Species described as common throughout the Chihuahuan Desert may be rare or absent in a particular area, and rare species may be locally abundant in some areas.

Most entries also have a **Comments** section, which provides information about closely related species, historical uses for the plant, and other interesting facts. Several plants in this book, according to other sources, have been eaten or used as medicine. Such information is recounted here for historical perspective only. Because of probable inaccuracies in early reports, and the potential for misidentification and confusion with poisonous "look-alikes," these plants should not be eaten or used medicinally.

Please practice "leave no trace" wildflower study. Leave the plants as you found them for others to enjoy.

WARNING

Ingesting plants or plant parts poses an extreme human health hazard and could result in sickness or even death. No one should attempt to use any wild plant for food or medicine without adequate training by a fully qualified professional. The author, publisher, and all others associated with the production and distribution of this book assume no liability for the actions of the reader.

CACTI AND OTHER SUCCULENTS

*This section includes plants with ribbed or
jointed succulent stems that are covered with
short or long spines growing from clusters.
Stems are either pad-shaped or cylindrical
and grow in joint-like branches or as single
or moundforming stems in a wide variety of
shapes. Other plants in this section have
long, sharp-pointed succulent leaves forming
rosettes from 1-20 feet (.9-6.1 m) high.*

RICK LOBELLO

Texas false-agave.

TEXAS FALSE-AGAVE
Hechtia texensis
Pineapple Family (Bromeliaceae)

Description: Texas false-agave resembles lechuguilla, with which it often grows. Texas false-agave can be distinguished by its fleshier and more recurved and pointed leaves, generally covered with red splotches in fall and winter. This succulent grows in groups up to 3' (1 m) across and blooms from February through May.

Habitat/Range: Texas false-agave is a curious-looking plant found only locally in our area. It can be abundant where found and generally occurs on limestone. It is most easily seen along the Rio Grande in Big Bend National Park and in adjacent Mexico. BBNP.

Comments: This species is the only member of the pineapple family in our area.

Sotol.

GEORGE O. MILLER

SOTOL

Dasylirion leiophyllum
Agave Family (Agavaceae)

Description: Sotol or desert candle is a characteristic plant of the northern Chihuahuan Desert, distinguished by incurved spines on long, slender, narrow leaves growing from a central clump. The plant produces a tall stalk up to 13' (4 m) high, having as many as 50,000 seeds.

Habitat/Range: BBNP, CCNP, GMNP.

Comments: Sotol flowers from May to August, with the flowering stalk an important source of nutrition for insects. Native Americans roasted the heart of the plant in mescal pits and ate it. More recently, the heart has been fermented to produce a liquor called sotol. The plant is widely used as an ornamental.

BRENT WAUER

Beargrass.

BEARGRASS
Nolina micrantha
Agave Family (Agavaceae)

Description: Although not a grass, this and similar species often resemble grasses. A low-growing perennial, beargrass can be locally common but is generally widespread only in low numbers. Flowers are purplish-tinged.

Habitat/Range: The taxonomy and distribution in this area are not well documented or understood. Beargrass occurs most frequently on limestone soils. CCNP, GMNP.

Comments: Domestic animals rarely feed on beargrass, which supposedly can be poisonous. Native Americans wove baskets and mats from the fibers. Another common name is sacahuiste.

RICK LOBELLO

Texas sacahuiste.

TEXAS SACAHUISTE
Nolina texana
Agave Family (Agavaceae)

Description: The flowers lack the purple tinge as in beargrass, and the main flower stalk is much more rigid.

Habitat/Range: This species is found in much of the same area and habitat as beargrass. BBNP, CCNP, GMNP.

Comments: Also known as bunchgrass.

BRENT WAUER

Banana yucca.

BANANA YUCCA
Yucca baccata
Agave Family (Agavaceae)

Description: As a group, yuccas are generally widespread in the northern Chihuahuan Desert and are often the most obvious large plant. In *Yucca baccata*, the leaves are very thick, and the trunk is usually stout but short. This species flowers from April to June and rarely at other times of the year when temperature and moisture are adequate.

Habitat/Range: Also known as datil, the plants occur in rocky areas throughout our region. CCNP, GMNP, WSNM.

Comments: The edible large fruits, which look something like bananas, were eaten by Native Americans. The fresh flowers are also edible, and leaf fibers are used to make baskets and similar items.

SOAPTREE YUCCA
Yucca elata
Agave Family (Agavaceae)

Description: Some individuals may reach a height of 13' (4 m) or more. The loose, peeling fibers on the leaf margins serve as a good identifying characteristic. It is most easily identified by its yellow leaf margins and lack of curly fibers peeling away from the leaf.

Habitat/Range: This narrow, thin-leafed yucca is common to abundant at lower elevations throughout the region. BBNP, CCNP, GMNP, WSNM.

Comments: Soaptree yucca increases dramatically in overgrazed areas, but often then gradually declines. The cream-colored blooms are visited by many insects; livestock occasionally eat the blossoms as well. When big enough, the trunk is used as a nest site by cavity-nesting birds such as ash-throated flycatchers and ladder-backed woodpeckers. The common name refers to our ability to obtain an equivalent of soap from the roots, which was used to shampoo hair.

BRENT WAUER

Soaptree yucca.

FAXON YUCCA
Yucca faxoniana
Agave Family (Agavaceae)

Description: This is the largest yucca in the northern Chihuahuan Desert, reaching a height of 29' (9 m). It is identified by its having saw-toothed to smooth edges on the leaves as opposed to the peeling fibers on the edges on soaptree yucca.

Habitat/Range: Faxon yucca occurs in rocky areas and can be locally common. Widely used as an ornamental, this plant is one most first-time visitors notice along roadsides in western Texas. BBNP, GMNP.

Comments: All the yuccas in this region are pollinted by moths in the genus *Tegeticula*, which are the same color as the petals of the flowers. Plants and insects have evolved a balanced, symbiotic relationship because the plant also feeds the insect and gives it a place to reproduce.

Faxon yucca.

TORREY YUCCA
Yucca treculeana
Agave Family (Agavaceae)

Description: This is a large, often common yucca. The plant is usually less than 6 ½' (2 m) tall, and that serves as the best distinguishing characteristic from other heavy-leafed yuccas. Formerly called *Yucca torreyi*.

Habitat/Range: BBNP, CCNP, GMNP.

Comments: Also known as Spanish dagger.

Torrey yucca.

RICK LOBELLO

Lechuguilla.

LECHUGUILLA
Agave lechuguilla
Agave Family (Agavaceae)

Description: Thick leaves with recurved spines growing from the base identify it readily.

Habitat/Range: Lechuguilla is the indicator plant of the Chihuahuan Desert, wholly restricted to this area. At middle and lower elevations it is often the dominant species, but its low stature can make it inconspicuous. This agave spreads through rhizomes and often occurs in extensive colonies. It is especially abundant in areas that have been overgrazed. BBNP, CCNP, GMNP.

Comments: After storing nutrients from three to thirty years, the plant grows a flower stalk 6-16' (2-5 m) tall in one tremendous spurt that lasts only a few weeks. After flowering, the plant usually dies. It blooms from April to August. Native Americans roasted the heart and stalk.

NEW MEXICO AGAVE
Agave neomexicana
Agave Family (Agavaceae)

Description: The leaves are much more robust and compact than those of lechuguilla and form a rosette that can be 2' (60 cm) across. The leaves are a deep bluish green.

Habitat/Range: This is the large agave found at higher elevations in the Guadalupe Mountains. It occurs at lower elevations also but is generally less common there than is lechuguilla. CCNP, GMNP.

Comments: Also known as maguey or century plant, the plant blooms from June to August and, like other agaves, does so only once in its life. This single blooming period follows 20 to 40 years of storing nutrients. The flowers are an important source of nectar for hummingbirds, grosbeaks, orioles, and other birds, and the seeds are gathered by many rodents. Native Americans also roasted the heart of this plant in mescal pits and wove the plant fibers into mats, ropes, and sandals. The plant is widely used as an ornamental.

BRENT WAUER

New Mexico agave.

Havard agave.

HAVARD AGAVE
Agave havardiana
Agave Family (Agavaceae)

Description: This is the large agave found in the southern part of our range.

Habitat/Range: It occurs in rocky areas with good drainage, especially in stands of grass. BBNP, GMNP.

Comments: It may take as many as 20 years for the plant to reach maturity and flower. Like other agaves, Havard agave spreads by rhizomes and can occur in thick stands. Also known as century plant. In Mexico, agaves are used to produce alcoholic beverages, such as mescal, pulque, and tequila.

NPS PHOTO

Candelilla.

CANDELILLA
Euphorbia antisyphilitica
Spurge Family (Euphorbiaceae)

Description: The thick clusters of leafless stems and the slender, erect growth suggest a horsetail or a rush at first glance. The flowers, growing near the tips of the stems, are white with a red center. Flowers appear from May through October.

Habitat/Range: This is a fairly common spurge on rocky slopes at lower elevations in Big Bend National Park. It often grows with sotol and lechuguilla. BBNP.

Comments: Candelilla was once a plant of great economic importance in the Chihuahuan Desert, especially along the Rio Grande. The stems still furnish carnauba wax, which has been used to make insulation, phonograph records, candles, and polishes. Juices of the plant were once used to treat venereal diseases but without any known benefit. It has been eliminated from much of its historic range because of overexploitation. Also known as wax plant.

GEORGE O. MILLER

Ocotillo.

OCOTILLO
Fouquieria splendens
Ocotillo Family (Fouquieriaceae)

Description: A single stem can be 9' (3 m) tall, but more commonly up to 6 ½' (2 m). When leaves are not present, photosynthesis takes place along the long, thorn-covered stem. But when a rain comes, the leaves, in arrested growth in buds, rapidly expand and transform the plant into fresh green. Bright red flowers bloom most frequently from April through June, but with plentiful moisture they can appear into late fall.

Habitat/Range: Ocotillo is an obvious plant at lower elevations in much of the Trans-Pecos area; it is especially common throughout limestone foothills and similar dry areas at Carlsbad Caverns, Guadalupe Mountains, and Big Bend. BBNP, CCNP, GMNP, WSNM.

Comments: The flowers attract many birds and insects, and deer browse the plant. Ocotillo is a popular ornamental, and many are removed from the desert for that purpose. Because it sprouts readily from cuttings, ocotillo is also often used as a "living fence."

GEORGE O. MILLER

Living rock.

LIVING ROCK
Ariocarpus fissuratus
Cactus Family (Cactaceae)

Description: This interesting cactus is often overlooked because of its low-growing habit and gray-green, rocklike appearance. The white to pink flower is conspicuous on the flat cap of the cactus.

Habitat/Range: The species prefers rocky, barren slopes and does not do well in shaded or moist areas. A thorough search, however, shows it to be locally common. Living rock occurs in Big Bend National Park and adjoining land, especially near the Rio Grande. BBNP.

Comments: Living rock cactus is often popular among collectors, but its ability to blend in with the environment has kept it from being eliminated over much of its range.

Turk's head.

TURK'S HEAD
Ferocactus haematacanthus
Cactus Family (Cactaceae)

Description: This large barrel cactus has striking large yellow flowers that have red-streaked petals. The flowers often cover the top of the plant.

Habitat/Range: It often grows in large clusters on cliffs, primarily along the Rio Grande in our area. In area parks, Turk's head is known only in Big Bend, where it blooms from May to July depending on moisture and temperature. BBNP.

Comments: Also known as *visnaga*.

COOKIE BALLOU

Devil's head.

DEVIL'S HEAD
Echinocactus horizonthalonius
Cactus Family (Cactaceae)

Description: This plant grows low to the ground, first in a globe shape but eventually forming a dome with rows of recurved spines. The flower is bright red to pink.

Habitat/Range: Devil's head can almost be described as common in many places, yet it is often overlooked. It is found most frequently on limestone soils along ridgetops. BBNP, CCNP, GMNP, WSNM.

Comments: Also known as *bisnagre.*

RO WAUER

Horse crippler.

HORSE CRIPPLER
Echinocactus texensis
Cactus Family (Cactaceae)

Description: Horse crippler's low-growing habit helps shelter it from cold. Plants can be up to 1' (0.3 m) across and grow on a variety of soil types. Spines on this plant are few but stout, thus the name horse crippler. Small but showy flowers often cover a large portion of the head of the plant. The pink to almost white, somewhat fragrant flowers are visited by many insects. The large red fruits swell and eventually break open, revealing an abundance of seeds.

Habitat/Range: This cactus grows low to the ground, so it is sometimes easy to miss. BBNP, CCNP, GMNP.

Comments: Harvester ants feed heavily on the ripened fruit. Also known as *manco caballo* (horse crippler).

RO WAUER

Green-flowered torch cactus.

GREEN-FLOWERED TORCH CACTUS
Echinocereus chloranthus
Cactus Family (Cactaceae)

Description: The flowers are variable and unusual in color, greenish to reddish brown, and can appear anywhere along the stem. As with many species of cactus, the flowers persist for only a few days but when present give the plant a distinctive appearance.

Habitat/Range: This is a locally common species, generally found in rocky or gravelly areas, especially limestone. If it is growing in good stands of native grass, this cactus can be overlooked. BBNP, CCNP, GMNP.

Comments: Also known as green-flowered pitaya.

Green strawberry hedgehog.

GREEN STRAWBERRY HEDGEHOG

Echinocereus enneacanthus
Cactus Family (Cactaceae)

Description: This low-growing hedgehog cactus has long, cylindrical stems that either lie flat on the ground or rise and taper slightly. The rigid spines are few in each cluster. The large flowers, up to 3" (8 cm) wide, range from purplish red to magenta. The greenish brown fruits taste simliar to strawberries.

Habitat/Range: This cactus often grows under shrubs that serve as nurse plants. BBNP, CCNP, GMNP.

Comments: Also known as strawberry cactus and pitaya.

STEVE WEST

Claret-cup cactus.

CLARET-CUP CACTUS
Echinocereus triglochidiatus
Cactus Family (Cactaceae)

Description: Despite its large size, this hedgehog cactus can often be fairly inconspicuous when it is not in bloom. However, when the bright scarlet flowers cover large clumps of this cactus, it is easy to spot. The blooming period is very short and variable, depending on temperature and moisture. Most plants complete the flowering cycle in May but some do not bloom until June.

Habitat/Range: It grows especially well in rocky areas and cliff faces, less frequently in low, sandy soils throughout our area. A good place to see it is in Walnut Canyon in Carlsbad Caverns National Park. BBNP, CCNP, GMNP, WSNM.

Comments: Also known as strawberry hedgehog.

New Mexico rainbow cactus.

NEW MEXICO RAINBOW CACTUS
Echinocereus viridiflorus
Cactus Family (Cactaceae)

Description: Depending on the spine colors, the stem ranges from solid brown to greenish to varicolored, hence the name rainbow cactus. The large flowers are generally yellow but can also be greenish brown.

Habitat/Range: This cactus is common in rocky areas. BBNP, CCNP, GMNP.

Comments: Also known as green pitaya.

BRENT WAUER

Button cactus.

BUTTON CACTUS
Epithelantha micromeris
Cactus Family (Cactaceae)

Description: The roundish individuals can be found growing singly or in clumps. The very small pink to flesh-colored flowers mature into bright red fruits. The flowering period can be long for a cactus, stretching from May through late August.

Habitat/Range: The button cactus, though widespread, is often overlooked because it is small and tends to blend in with the surrounding limestone rock. BBNP, CCNP, GMNP.

Comments: Also known as *mulato*.

PLAIN LACE-SPINE CACTUS
Mammillaria lasiacantha
Cactus Family (Cactaceae)

Description: This is another tiny cactus, generally no more than 2" (5 cm) tall, that is often initially overlooked. The petals of the white flowers have a central red stripe. The flowering period is February through April. The abundant, thick growth of the white spines gives it the appearance of being covered with white lace.

Habitat/Range: It occurs primarily in limestone soils but may be obscured by grass cover. BBNP, CCNP, GMNP.

GEORGE O. MILLER

Plain lace-spine cactus.

Nipple cactus.

NIPPLE CACTUS
Mammillaria heyderi
Cactus Family (Cactaceae)

Description: You have to really look for this cactus, for it is not frequently encountered. Unlike most *Mammillaria*, the stem grows mostly underground, with the exposed part flat and almost level with the surface. Although this cactus may actually grow 6" (15 cm) or more in diameter, it is often overlooked. The flowers are variable, ranging from white to pink, and bloom from May through August.

Habitat/Range: BBNP, CCNP, GMNP.

Comments: Also known as pancake cactus.

Cane cholla.

CANE CHOLLA
Opuntia imbricata
Cactus Family (Cactaceae)

Description: Cane cholla is a common, obvious species in most of our area. New plants sprout from joints scattered from a parent, creating colonies of many plants of various heights, some taller than 6 ½' (2 m). The magenta flowers can cover the plant from May through August, with a few as late as early October.

Habitat/Range: BBNP, CCNP, GMNP, WSNM.

Comments: Deer eat the ripe, yellow fruit. Cane cholla provides important nesting sites for cactus wrens and curve-billed thrashers. The stems and fruit are occasionally eaten by cattle, and the joints take root easily in overgrazed areas.

BRENT WAUER

Christmas cactus.

CHRISTMAS CACTUS
Opuntia leptocaulis
Cactus Family (Cactaceae)

Description: This slender-stemmed plant often grows under other plants, and it can be common in overgrazed areas. The small greenish to yellow flowers are present in May and June. The long spines are often covered with sheaths, a characteristic of cholla. The fruit is an important winter food for scaled quail.

Habitat/Range: Although widespread throughout our area, Christmas cactus is often overlooked due to its spindly texture and shape. BBNP, CCNP, FDHS, GMNP, WSNM.

Comments: Also known as *tasajillo*.

GEORGE O. MILLER

Klein cholla.

KLEIN CHOLLA
Opuntia kleiniae
Cactus Family (Cactaceae)

Description: Highly variable in color, the flowers range from greenish to purple to pink. The species closely resembles the Christmas cactus, except the stems are thicker and the flower petals are a somewhat different color.

Habitat/Range: Klein cholla occurs in our area in low numbers, most often found in rocky soil, but also in silt. BBNP, CCNP, GMNP, WSNM.

NEW MEXICO PRICKLY PEAR
Opuntia phaeacantha
Cactus Family (Cactaceae)

Description: The translucent spines are reddish orange to brown. The bright golden-yellow flowers have red centers that often change to peach as the flowers mature. The blooming period is from April through August. The flowers are 2 ¾-3" (7-8 cm) across.

Habitat/Range: This is one of the more widespread pad *Opuntia* found in our area. It is often abundant in limestone areas but grows in various other soil types too, at low to middle elevations, less frequently at high elevations. BBNP, CCNP, GMNP, WSNM.

Comments: This species often predominates in overgrazed places. Many animals, including javelinas, rock squirrels, coyotes, and woodrats, eat the fruits, which provide much-needed moisture for them. Fruits, or tunas, of this and other prickly pears are eaten fresh and canned in Mexican cuisine. Also known as brown-spined prickly pear.

BRENT WAUER

New Mexico prickly pear.

GEORGE O. MILLER

Blind pear.

BLIND PEAR
Opuntia rufida
Cactus Family (Cactaceae)

Description: This species barely enters our area but is of interest because of the lack of spines. Though it lacks spines, it does possess an abundance of tiny, short, barbed glochids that protect the pads. Cattle have supposedly been blinded by the windblown glochids. This cactus often develops a trunk and can be over 5' (1.5 m) in height. The bright yellow flowers occur in April and May.

Habitat/Range: Blind pear is found along the Rio Grande from Big Bend National Park to Presidio, Texas, most commonly on rocky hillsides. BBNP.

RICK LOBELLO

Purple prickly pear.

PURPLE PRICKLY PEAR
Opuntia violacea
Cactus Family (Cactaceae)

Description: The reddish purple pigment in the pads draws immediate attention to this unique cactus. The purple color seems to predominate where it is hotter and drier, as in the Big Bend area, or where winters are long and dry. Many, however, have green pads and are best identified by the long spines, usually black and in groups of up to three. Flowers occur from April through August and are bright yellow with red centers.

Habitat/Range: This plant grows at lower elevations. BBNP, CCNP, GMNP, WSNM.

Comments: When other food sources are scarce, deer and javelina will feed on the pads. This species often is cataloged under a different scientific name, *Opuntia macrocentra*.

WHITE FLOWERS

This section includes flowers that are predominantly white. Since white flowers grade into both pale pink and pale blue flowers, and off-white flowers may appear yellowish, readers should check the pink and purple, blue, and yellow sections as well.

LAURENCE PARENT

Four-wing saltbush.

FOUR-WING SALTBUSH

Atriplex canescens
Goosefoot Family (Chenopodiaceae)

Description: A many-branched, erect shrub; individual plants can be over 6 ½' (2 m) in height but most are around 3' (1 m). Dry, four-winged seeds are present on female plants through most of the year. Plants flower from June to September.

Habitat/Range: This shrub occurs commonly and in a wide variety of soil types and habitats at lower elevations. BBNP, CCNP, FDHS, GMNP, WSNM.

Comments: Saltbush helps retard erosion and is persistent during drought. These hardy qualities have led to its use in reclaiming disturbed areas such as mine sites. Many mammals and birds eat the seeds. Overbrowsing by stock can kill the plant, but it can recover from limited grazing. Native Americans ground the dry seeds for use in bread making and to make a drink called pinole.

BRENT WAUER

Gyp ringstem.

GYP RINGSTEM
Anulocaulis gypsogenus
Four-O'Clock Family (Nyctaginaceae)

Description: This bizarre plant is easily identified by the large, coarse basal leaves, a height often in excess of 3' (1 m), and long, slender greenish white flowers with pink shading at the base of the flower. The flowers can be up to 1 ⅛" (3 cm) long and bloom from June to as late as November.

Habitat/Range: As the common name implies, this is a gyp-obligate species, occurring only in soils with a high gypsum content. GMNP.

Comments: The plant grows from a woody rootstock, and the stems have prominent sticky rings near the joints.

GEORGE O. MILLER

Western virgin's bower.

WESTERN VIRGIN'S BOWER
Clematis drummondii
Crowfoot Family (Ranunculaceae)

Description: The petals of the small cream-colored flowers are rudimentary or absent. The seeds persist on the vine through winter. This perennial climbing vine is usually not obvious until late summer through fall when silky fruits cover the plant. It blooms in August, with male and female flowers on separate plants.

Habitat/Range: Virgin's bower grows over fences and other plants, preferring well-drained soil in open areas. BBNP, CCNP, FDHS, GMNP.

Comments: Known locally as old man's beard, it makes an attractive fence cover and requires little water.

CHISOS PRICKLY POPPY
Argemone chisosensis
Poppy Family (Papaveraceae)

Description: The six petals of the flower range from white to deep pink and occur from March through June. The plant grows up to 3' (1 m) in height. All the leaves are lobed, especially the lower ones.

Habitat/Range: In our area, this plant's range is restricted to western Texas, although it also occurs in northern Mexico. Like other species of *Argemone,* the plant produces a yellow latex. It is found in a wide variety of habitats including open flats, roadsides, and well-drained areas. BBNP, CCNP, GMNP.

Comments: Also known as pink prickly poppy.

BETTY ALEX

Chisos prickly poppy.

CRESTED PRICKLY POPPY
Argemone polyanthemos
Poppy Family (Papaveraceae)

Description: Crested prickly poppy is a typical *Argemone*, producing yellow sap and having pale green leaves. The multibranched plant can be slightly more than 3' (1 m) in height. The leaf blades are broad and only slightly lobed, with the uppermost ones clasping the stem. The flowers, with their large white petals, occur from April through July, sometimes into early fall. The flowers are up to 2 ¾" (7 cm) wide, and the plant is covered with slender yellow prickles.

Habitat/Range: This annual or biennial is found in much of the northern area covered by this book. It occurs in sandy or gravelly soil, on both flat plains and slopes. CCNP, WSNM.

Comments: Strong alkaloids in *Argemone* cause most animals to avoid it, but doves feed heavily on the seeds and apparently are not affected.

Crested prickly poppy.

Desert prickly poppy.

DESERT PRICKLY POPPY
Argemone squarrosa
Poppy Family (Papaveraceae)

Description: Plants grow up to 2' (60 cm) in height. The blue-green, spine-tipped leaves are deeply lobed, clasp the stem, and covered with prickly bristles. The white flowers have numerous yellow stamens and are 2 ¾" (7 cm) across. It occurs in open areas and blooms from April through September. CCNP, FDHS, GMNP.

Habitat/Range: This perennial is found throughout lower elevations in west Texas and southeastern New Mexico.

Comments: As with other species of *Argemone*, a spiny fruit is produced.

RICK LOBELLO

Mountain peppergrass.

MOUNTAIN PEPPERGRASS
Lepidium montanum
Mustard Family (Brassicaceae)

Description: The plants usually appear as short, rarely more than 16" (40 cm) high, rounded bushes capped with white flowers. The flowers have four petals and bloom from March through late summer. Leaves are long and narrow, and the plant is many branched.

Habitat/Range: The common name for this plant is misleading, for it is found throughout the area, not just in mountains. In fact, it is generally more common in lowlands. Peppergrass is most often encountered in disturbed areas and is often conspicuous along roadsides. It is one of the first plants to reappear in burned areas. BBNP, CCNP, FDHS, GMNP, WSNM.

Comments: Several authors mention it as good deer browse. The seeds are peppery tasting and when dried can be used as a seasoning on food.

Velvety nerisyrenia.

VELVETY NERISYRENIA
Greggia camporum
Mustard Family (Brassicaceae)

Description: The leaves are spatula-shaped to broadly lance-shaped and toothed, on plants that are 8-24" (20-60 cm) tall. The flowers are among the first blooms of the year, appearing as early as January and continuing into November. They are about ¾" (2 cm) wide. In only a day or so, the white flowers change to rose or lavender.

Habitat/Range: This species is most likely found in lower-elevation grassland and desert, in limestone or limestone-derived soils. BBNP, CCNP, WSNM.

Comments: This perennial mustard, also known as greggia, initially appears whitish or grayish due to the hairiness of the plant.

COOKIE BALLOU

Narrowleaf greggia.

NARROWLEAF GREGGIA
Greggia linearifolia
Mustard Family (Brassicaceae)

Description: This species is similar to *Greggia camporum*, except it is not as hairy and the leaves are linear rather than spatula-shaped. The plant is in bloom from April to August.

Habitat/Range: Greggia is found primarily on gypsum soils such as at White Sands National Monument. BBNP, CCNP, GMNP, WSNM.

CLAMMYWEED
Polanisia dodecandra
Caper Family (Capparidaceae)

Description: A strong-smelling plant, clammyweed is covered with moist, sticky glands. Stems are simple or branched, and leaves are alternate. The plant grows up to 2' (60 cm) in height. It bears white to cream-colored flowers from April through October.

Habitat/Range: This annual occurs in open areas including sandy slopes, flats, along arroyos, and even into pinyon-juniper woodland. CCNP.

GEORGE O. MILLER

Clammyweed.

Cliff fendlerbush.

LEWIS EPPLE

CLIFF FENDLERBUSH
Fendlera rupicola
Saxifrage Family (Saxifragaceae)

Description: Cliff fendlerbush is a widely branched shrub that grows up to 6 ½' (2 m) in height. The leaves are opposite and are lance-shaped to elliptic; the leaf margins curl under. Furrowed gray bark is also characteristic of fendlerbush. The four-petaled flowers are large, nearly ½" (1.3 cm) wide, occurring either singly or in clusters of two or three. The flowers, with eight stamens, are white to purple tinged. They bloom from March to June, occasionally as late as August.

Habitat/Range: Found in rocky, well-drained areas that receive generous sunlight, in wooded canyons, and even on cliff faces of both limestone and igneous rock. This drought resister appears at elevations from 3018' (920 m) up to 7874' (2400 m). BBNP, CCNP, GMNP.

Comments: Fendlerbush is frequently browsed by deer and goats.

LEWIS EPPLE

Hitchcock mockorange.

HITCHCOCK MOCKORANGE
Philadelphus hitchcockianus
Saxifrage Family (Saxifragaceae)

Description: This is a small shrub, only about 27" (70 cm) tall. The leaves are ovate. Fragrant, solitary, white flowers, blooming from May through August, have more than 20 stamens each. As with littleleaf mockorange, the bark peels off readily.

Habitat/Range: This plant seems to be restricted in our area to the Guadalupe Mountains. It prefers rocky locales on canyon walls and bottoms. CCNP, GMNP.

Comments: Littleleaf mockorange *(Philodelphus microphyllus)* often occurs at a higher elevation and has more ovate leaves.

APACHE PLUME
Fallugia paradoxa
Rose Family (Rosaceae)

Description: The silvery tufted fruits, or "plumes," give Apache plume its common name. Apache plume forms clumps, and individual plants usually do not exceed 6 ½' (2 m) in height. Along with the tufted fruits, the white flowers, in bloom from February to October, aid in identification.

Habitat/Range: Favored habitat is in the bottoms of rocky canyons such as Walnut Canyon, where it is often dominant. BBNP, CCNP, GMNP.

Comments: Apache plume serves as good browse for deer, especially in winter when other foods become scarce. It is good for erosion control and makes a nice ornamental. Also known as *ponil.*

COOKIE BALLOU

Apache plume.

Southwestern chokecherry.

SOUTHWESTERN CHOKECHERRY
Prunus serotina
Rose Family (Rosaceae)

Description: In our area, this species can reach the size of a small tree, usually less than 19' (6 m) tall. Leaves are oval-oblong to lance-shaped with serrated margins. Blooms are present from April to June. The white to pink flowers grow in showy spikes. The red fruit, which eventually turns purplish, is present from July through August, or until it is all eaten by many species of birds and mammals.

Habitat/Range: A wide-ranging species, southwestern chokecherry occurs throughout our area at middle elevations along arroyos and streams. BBNP, CCNP, FDHS, GMNP.

GEORGE O. MILLER

Gregg's catclaw.

GREGG'S CATCLAW
Acacia greggii
Legume Family (Fabaceae)

Description: White or yellowish flowers on short spikes appear from May to August. The seedpods are flat, linear, and constricted between the seeds. The thick spines bend backward.

Habitat/Range: Gregg's catclaw is a small tree or shrub generally widespread in the northern Chihuahuan Desert at elevations up to 4921' (1500 m). BBNP, CCNP, GMNP.

Comments: Because of its thick spines, Gregg's catclaw is resistant to heavy grazing.

ROEMER ACACIA
Acacia roemeriana
Legume Family (Fabaceae)

Description: Leaflets are strongly veined and hairless, and are longer than in other acacias. The creamy-white flower heads, about ⅜" (1 cm) across, bloom in spring, or later, if soil moisture is adequate. The pods are long, up to 4" (10 cm), and they are flat rather than constricted between the seeds as in Gregg's catclaw.

Habitat/Range: Roemer acacia reaches the northern limits of its range near Carlsbad, but otherwise it is found at lower elevations south into Mexico. BBNP, CCNP, GMNP.

Comments: Like the other types of legumes, this is a valuable honey plant.

JEAN HARDY

Roemer acacia.

PRAIRIE ACACIA
Acacia texensis
Legume Family (Fabaceae)

Description: This unspined acacia spreads through rhizomes, forming colonies of shrubs less than 1' (30 cm) tall. The leaflets are narrow. Fragrant cream-colored flowers are present from May through August.

Habitat/Range: More than other acacias, this species is likely to be found in sandy areas, but it also grows in rocky ground, at elevations up to 6562' (2000 m). BBNP, FDHS.

Comments: Also known as whiteball acacia.

Prairie acacia.

CATCLAW MIMOSA
Mimosa biuncifera
Legume Family (Fabaceae)

Description: This plant grows 3-6 ½' (1-2 m) tall, preferring dry, rocky areas on both limestone and igneous rock. The plant has recurved claws with leaves of four to eight pairs of segments. The round, cream-colored flower heads are about ½" (1.3 cm) across.

Habitat/Range: Catclaw mimosa is a common shrub at low to middle elevations in the northern Chihuahuan Desert. BBNP, CCNP, FDHS, GMNP.

Comments: This plant, also known as *estraellita* (small star), is occasionally browsed by deer and is a favorite plant for bees.

Catclaw mimosa.

BRENT WAUER

Mexican orange.

MEXICAN ORANGE
Choisya dumosa
Citrus Family (Rutaceae)

Description: This plant can reach up to 3' (1 m) in height. The coarsely toothed leaves and the citrus odor of the crushed leaves are the easiest ways to identify the plant. The white flowers, which are less than ¾" (2 cm) long, occur from June to as late as November.

Habitat/Range: The strong-scented Mexican orange, an evergreen shrub, is often quite common in rocky drainages and other rocky sites throughout our area. CCNP, GMNP.

Comments: Also known as *zorrillo* (skunk).

LEATHERSTEM
Jatropha dioica
Spurge Family (Euphorbiaceae)

Description: The leaves are alternate or clustered and are shed after the first cold weather or during dry periods. Stems are reddish and flexible, growing in clusters sometimes up to 27" (70 cm) tall. The small, white flowers have five fused sepals. They may bloom from May to October. The seeds are large, about ⅜" (1 cm) in diameter.

Habitat/Range: This plant is most common near the Rio Grande, especially on limestone slopes. A small, isolated population of this species occurs on the west side of Guadalupe Mountains National Park, and it is generally common in low areas of Big Bend National Park. BBNP, GMNP.

Comments: Rubber has been extracted from the stems, and the roots contain tannin and produce a red dye. The large seeds are a primary source of food in autumn for white-winged doves, and people also occasionally eat the seeds. Also known as *sangre de drago*.

RICK LOBELLO

Leatherstem.

Lanceleaf sumac.

LANCELEAF SUMAC
Rhus lanceolata
Sumac Family (Anacardiaceae)

Description: This is a shrub- to tree-sized plant up to 16' (5 m) tall. The long, slender, compound leaves occur in groups of 13 to 19. When the leaflets turn reddish purple in the fall, a thick stand of this plant is dazzling. The white flowers appear as terminal clusters from May to August. The red fruit is covered with small hairs.

Habitat/Range: BBNP, CCNP, GMNP.

Comments: Deer and many species of birds feed on the fruit.

BRENT WAUER

Western soapberry.

WESTERN SOAPBERRY
Sapindus saponaria
Soapberry Family (Sapindaceae)

Description: This plant is best identified by the evenly pinnate leaves; the translucent, round, amber fruit; and the large white clusters of flowers blooming from April to August. In many ways soapberry resembles the Chinaberry *(Melia azedarach).* It can grow to 33' (10 m) high, but most trees in our area are about half that height.

Habitat/Range: This widespread, southwestern tree is locally common along streams and arroyos in the northern Chihuahuan Desert, almost always growing in groups. A large stand is found at Rattlesnake Springs at CCNP, along the road between the picnic and the housing area. BBNP, CCNP, FDHS, GMNP.

Comments: Birds use the tree for nesting, and many species feed on the seeds in the fall. A fast grower, soapberry makes a good windbreak. The common name comes from the lather produced by the seeds. In Mexico, where it is called *jaboncillo* (small soap), it is sometimes used to wash clothes.

DESERT CEANOTHUS
Ceanothus greggii
Buckthorn Family (Rhamnaceae)

Description: This is a leafy shrub, reaching about 6 ½' (2 m) in height, with short, rigid branches. White flowers appear at the ends or the axils of the branches in March through at least June. The leaves are opposite.

Habitat/Range: Desert ceanothus grows in canyons or on rocky slopes. CCNP, GMNP.

Comments: This species is good browse for elk and deer, while chipmunks and various birds reportedly eat the seeds. In Mexico, people obtain red dyes from the roots, and the flowers can be agitated in water to produce a cleansing lather.

LEWIS EPPLE

Desert ceanothus.

PRAIRIE EVENING PRIMROSE
Oenothera albicaulis
Evening Primrose Family (Onagraceae)

Description: This species is similar to white evening primrose, except prairie evening primrose is an annual. From April to early July, the large white flowers are in bloom, the petals fading to pink as the flower matures. The flowers open late in the afternoon and close an hour or two after daybreak.

Habitat/Range: This species occurs in loose soils and disturbed areas. BBNP, CCNP, FDHS, GMNP, WSNM.

Comments: Native Americans had several medicinal uses for the various evening primroses, including preparing a tea to treat kidney pains.

Prairie evening primrose.

WHITE EVENING PRIMROSE
Oenothera pallida
Evening Primrose Family (Onagraceae)

Description: Like prairie evening primrose, the flowers of this species also have large, white petals that gradually fade to pink. The flowers open completely in just a half hour in the evening, with sudden visible jerks. The blooming period is from April to September, occasionally as late as October.

Habitat/Range: White evening primrose occurs most frequently in open areas and along roadsides, especially where the surface has been disturbed. CCNP, GMNP, WSNM.

Comments: The pollen is sticky, and when a visiting moth touches the anthers they release cobwebby strings of pollen that stick on the moth, which then transports it to another flower. This perennial spreads from rootstocks, while prairie evening primrose is an annual.

White evening primrose.

GEORGE O. MILLER

Western water hemlock.

WESTERN WATER HEMLOCK
Cicuta maculata
Parsley Family (Apiaceae)

Description: On the tops of the plants, which can reach 6 ½' (2 m) in height, are umbels of numerous white to greenish white flowers. The flowers bloom from May through September and occasionally as late as October. Stout, hollow stems and pinnately compound leaves with sawtooth edges help identify it.

Habitat/Range: Western water hemlock can be locally common in wet areas, and it is especially abundant along Rattlesnake Creek in Carlsbad Caverns National Park. CCNP.

Comments: This is a POISONOUS plant, reported to be deadly to cattle as well as to humans. Do not mistake it for wild parsnip; leave it alone. Also known as cowbane.

HORSETAIL MILKWEED
Asclepias subverticillata
Milkweed Family (Asclepiadaceae)

Description: Horsetail milkweed is easily identified by the linear, whorled leaves and white flowers. It can be up to 3' (1 m) tall.

Habitat/Range: It occurs widely in limestone soils. BBNP, CCNP, FDHS, GMNP, WSNM.

Comments: This species is highly poisonous to livestock. Dried plants retain several toxins and resins, giving it another common name, rosin milkweed.

BRENT WAUER

Horsetail milkweed.

FRAGRANT HELIOTROPE
Heliotropium greggii
Borage Family (Boraginaceae)

Description: The leaves are covered with tiny hairs, and the stems are usually numerous and prostrate. The sweet-smelling white flowers with slightly yellow centers occur from May to October. They are funnel-shaped and less than ½" (1.3 cm) across. The coiled inflorescence of the borage and waterleaf families distinguishes these two from all other plant families in the region.

Habitat/Range: Fragrant heliotrope is a locally common perennial that forms colonies of plants on calcareous soils through much of our area. BBNP, CCNP, GMNP, WSNM.

Comments: Also known as Gregg's heliotrope.

Fragrant heliotrope.

WHITEBRUSH
Aloysia wrightii
Vervain Family (Lamiaceae)

Description: Whitebrush is a common shrub ranging up to 6 ½' (2 m) in height, but usually only to about 27" (69 cm). The slender, hairy branches bear simple, oval to roundish leaves with evenly toothed margins. Small, white, aromatic flowers with tubular calyxes bloom in April and May.

Habitat/Range: This species is commonly found in arroyos, rocky canyons, and on slopes. BBNP, CCNP, FDHS, GMNP.

Comments: Bees depend heavily on this plant and produce good honey from the nectar. Cattle also feed on this plant. Also known as beebrush and *oreganillo*.

Whitebrush.

BARTON WARNOCK

Jimsonweed.

JIMSONWEED
Datura meteloides
Nightshade Family (Solanaceae)

Description: This plant is erect, up to 27" (70 cm) high, with dark green, ovate leaves. The large white flowers show traces of violet or lavender on the petals and bloom from June to September. The fruiting body is green, musty smelling, and covered with spines, which explains another common name, thornapple.

Habitat/Range: Jimsonweed is a poisonous but attractive plant found at lower elevations in our area, in sandy loose soils or in floodplains. BBNP, FDHS, WSNM.

Comments: Hawk moths, bees, beetles, and hummingbirds pollinate the flowers. Jimsonweed contains the drug atropine and various alkaloids and is highly toxic to people and livestock. Also known as Wright thornapple.

RED DEVIL'S CLAW
Proboscidea parviflora
Unicorn Plant Family (Martyniaceae)

Description: A large, two-lipped flower blooms from April to October, although June through September is most typical. The striking flower is reddish purple to almost white with streaks of yellow. The heart-shaped leaves are another identifying mark. The fruit resembles an okra pod, is reported to be edible, and is also used in Native American basketry. The mature seedpod splits into two, and each part has a long curved hook.

Habitat/Range: This interesting plant occurs in scattered lowland locations, especially washes and rocky soils throughout our area. BBNP, CCNP.

Comments: The hooks can catch on the leg of a passing animal and thus help disperse the seeds. This hook is the origin of the common name devil's claw. Also known as New Mexico devil's claw. A similar species, *P. arenaria*, is more likely to occur in sandy areas and is a perennial.

GEORGE O. MILLER

Red devil's claw.

BRENT WAUER

Western white honeysuckle.

WESTERN WHITE HONEYSUCKLE
Lonicera albiflora
Honeysuckle Family (Caprifoliaceae)

Description: This woody shrub, which reaches 6 ½-9' (2-3 m) in height, is most frequently found in moist limestone canyons, twining through other plants. Most populations have white flowers and are not hairy, but variety *dumosa* has hairy leaves and stems. Occasionally yellowish white flowers are found. Flowers bloom most frequently in the spring but sometimes are noted into early fall. The bright red fruits are translucent. Most western white honeysuckle resembles, at least initially, the common Japanese honeysuckle *(Lonicera japonica)* of urban areas.

Habitat/Range: This species occurs at lower elevations than does Arizona honeysuckle. BBNP, CCNP, FDHS, GMNP.

Comments: Many species of birds eat the berries, and deer feed on the plant.

Seepwillow baccharis.

SEEPWILLOW BACCHARIS
Baccharis glutinosa
Sunflower Family (Asteraceae)

Description: This plant often forms thickets, with individual plants growing up to 13' (4 m) in height. The simple, alternate leaves are long, slender, and willowlike. Flowers occur from May through September.

Habitat/Range: This shrub is generally fairly common along watercourses and similar riparian areas. Although baccharis may grow some distance from water, its presence is usually an indication of at least subsurface water. BBNP, CCNP, WSNM.

Comments: This is an important plant in erosion control, and many animals use it as food. Native Americans of this region reportedly used the straight stems for arrow shafts.

SPREADING FLEABANE
Erigeron divergens
Sunflower Family (Asteraceae)

Description: Spreading fleabane is a well-branched perennial that rarely exceeds 27" (69 cm) in height. The plant is covered with stiff hairs. The upper stem leaves are slender, and the ones at the bottom of the plant are pinnate. The flowers are variable, but most have white ray flowers that may also be pink, lavender, or even bluish. More than 100 ray flowers can be layered around the yellow disk flowers. This species blooms from March to October.

Habitat/Range: This species occurs in open areas at all elevations. CCNP, GMNP.

Spreading fleabane.

WHITE-EYE GOLDENWEED
Machaeranthera blephariphylla
Sunflower Family (Asteraceae)

Description: Normally several stems grow from a woody base, and the leaves are serrated, with 20 to 30 teeth. The ray flowers are whitish, sometimes having a hint of pink or light violet on the undersurface; the disk flowers are yellow. The flowering period extends from June to October with adequate fall rains.

Habitat/Range: This perennial herb is found throughout our area at middle to high elevations. BBNP, CCNP, GMNP.

BRENT WAUER

White-eye goldenweed.

JEAN HARDY

Plains blackfoot.

PLAINS BLACKFOOT
Melampodium leucanthum
Sunflower Family (Asteraceae)

Description: Plains blackfoot is a low-growing composite, many branched with linear to oblong leaves. Plants grow in a clump and are usually less than 6" (15 cm) tall and 16" (40 cm) across. The ray flowers are white and sometimes have purple veins on the underside of the petals. The disk flowers are yellow. Blooming is from April to October. This plant is similar to desert zinnia, except desert zinnia has fewer petals and they do not completely surround the disk.

Habitat/Range: Plains blackfoot occurs in rocky outcrops and in dry limestone soils. BBNP, CCNP, GMNP.

Guayule.

GUAYULE
Parthenium argentatum
Sunflower Family (Asteraceae)

Description: A composite, guayule produces cream-colored flowers on bare stalks after summer rains in July and August. The stems are flexible, and the leaves are toothed and grayish. It usually grows less than 3' (1 m) high.

Habitat/Range: This species is most easily found in Big Bend National Park, where it can be locally common. Through the rest of the southern part of the Big Bend region, it occurs widely but is generally not common. This perennial shrub normally grows in predominantly limestone areas at elevations from 2625' (800 m) to 4593' (1400 m). BBNP.

Comments: A high-quality rubber is produced in the stem and root tissues of guayule. The first attempt at commercial exploitation occurred in Mexico in 1892, and other efforts were made in the Southwest, including during World War II when traditional supplies of rubber were cut off.

MARIOLA
Parthenium incanum
Sunflower Family (Asteraceae)

Description: A perennial, mariola occurs as a small shrub, up to 27" (69 cm) tall. The plant is many branched and shrubby at the base. It is covered with many small grayish leaves. This plant flowers from July to October, and the leaves give off a pleasant odor when crushed.

Habitat/Range: Mariola is often common throughout our area at low to middle elevations and is most often found in limestone soils in dry areas. BBNP, CCNP, FDHS, GMNP.

Comments: This plant contains rubber, as does guayule. Attempts to cross the two to obtain a cold-tolerant plant have not succeeded. Mariola is infrequently grazed by livestock, and thick stands of it indicate previous overgrazing.

Mariola.

PINK AND PURPLE FLOWERS

*This section includes flowers ranging from
pink to purple or shades in between. Some bluish
plants may be in this section, but be sure to also
check the blue flower section.*

BRENT WAUER

Nodding onion.

NODDING ONION
Allium cernuum
Lily Family (Liliaceae)

Description: The umbel of pinkish white, bell-like flowers readily identifies this species, as does the distinctive shepherd's crook stalk supporting the umbel. The plants often grow in groups.

Habitat/Range: Many members of this genus are found in our area. This species occurs across much of North America as far south as Mexico and as far east as Georgia. Nodding onion can be found at higher elevations, above 4921' (1500 m). BBNP, CCNP, GMNP.

Comments: The small bulbs can be responsibly collected and used for flavoring, and many animals, including Montezuma quail, feed heavily on the bulbs.

UMBRELLA-WORT
Allionia incarnata
Four-O'Clock Family (Nyctaginaceae)

Description: Umbrella-wort is a creeper with stems 3' (1 m) to rarely 9' (3 m) in length. Plants bloom from April to September, occasionally as late as October. The flower is actually a cluster of three flowers, which are purple to deep pink in color.

Habitat/Range: This is a conspicuous perennial of open, dry areas. BBNP, CCNP, GMNP, WSNM.

Comments: They open at sunrise and generally close by midday except when it is overcast. The fruits are noticeably toothed and have perpetually sticky stalked glands in the groove between the rows of hooked teeth. Doves eat the fruits. Grains of sand often cling to the sticky stems. Known in Spanish as *hierba de la hormiga* (ant plant.)

Umbrella-wort.

NARROWLEAF SPIDERLING
Boerhavia linearifolia
Four-O'Clock Family (Nyctaginaceae)

Description: This perennial is low growing, up to 23" (59 cm) in length. The dark purple-red flowers, with five lobes, bloom from June through September. The stems are brittle at the joints.

Habitat/Range: The plant grows in dry soil and on rocky cliffs, often at canyon mouths in the Guadalupe Mountains. CCNP, GMNP.

Narrowleaf spiderling.

BRENT WAUER

Leatherflower.

LEATHERFLOWER
Clematis filifera
Crowfoot Family (Ranunculaceae)

Description: This *Clematis* vine produces bell-like flowers in excess of 3/4" (2 cm) across, blooming from April through September.

Habitat/Range: The plant grows throughout our area mostly above 4265' (1300 m) in elevation, in rocky canyons and along canyon walls. BBNP, GMNP, CCNP.

Comments: Leatherflower climbs over other plants or boulders. It is browsed by deer.

WHITE LARKSPUR
Delphinium virescens
Crowfoot Family (Ranunculaceae)

Description: The stems are stout and erect, with the plant commonly growing up to 1' (30 cm) tall. Flowers occur only on the upper half to upper third of the plant, most of them white but occasionally light blue to greenish. The flowers are about 1" (2.5 cm) wide, and the upper sepal is prominently spurred. It blooms from April through July.

Habitat/Range: This widespread perennial herb is found throughout our area at low to middle elevations but is usually only locally common. This species occurs in dry areas including plains, hillsides, and grasslands. GMNP.

Comments: Also known as plains larkspur.

BRENT WAUER

White larkspur.

PURPLE LOCOWEED
Astragalus missouriensis
Legume Family (Fabaceae)

Description: Purple locoweed is a perennial herb with a taproot and prostrate stems. This plant has compound leaves with 9-17 leaflets per leaf. The leaflets are elliptical and covered with silver hairs. Bluish purple to violet flowers occur from March through June in short terminal heads. The straight seedpods form an elongated cylinder.

Habitat/Range: Locoweed is found locally in our area primarily in the Guadalupe and Glass Mountains and in desert grasslands from 3970' to 8530' (1500 m to 2300 m) elevation. CCNP.

Purple locoweed.

Woolly loco.

WOOLLY LOCO
Astragalus mollissimus
Legume Family (Fabaceae)

Description: The stems of this perennial herb are usually numerous, and the plant is no more than about 14" (35 cm) tall. The bad-smelling purple flowers occur as early as February; the plant keeps producing them through May. Leaves are alternate and pinnately compound, and the pods are strongly curved.

Habitat/Range: Woolly loco is more widespread than purple locoweed, growing on open plains and rocky slopes from 3970' to 8530' (1210 m to 2600 m). BBNP, CCNP, FDHS, GMNP.

Comments: Often green when everything else appears dead, this plant is sometimes consumed by livestock with fatal effects. Locoweed spreads on overgrazed and disturbed soils.

Feather dalea.

FEATHER DALEA
Dalea formosa
Legume Family (Fabaceae)

Description: Four of the five flower petals are rose color, while the fifth, the banner, begins as yellow then passes to maroon, possibly signaling to insects that the flower has probably already been pollinated and no longer has nectar to offer. The plant grows up to about 3' (1 m) tall and is covered with small leaves. Except when the dense clusters of flowers are in bloom from February to June, feather dalea is rather inconspicuous.

Habitat/Range: Although sometimes hard to locate, this is a common shrub on limestone ridgetops and canyon slopes at lower elevations. BBNP, CCNP, GMNP.

Comments: Deer browse the plant, and various rodents eat the seeds. Native Americans used an extract of it to dye plant fibers for baskets.

FRAGRANT MIMOSA
Mimosa borealis
Legume Family (Fabaceae)

Description: A shrub, fragrant mimosa grows up to 3' (1 m) tall. Leaves are compound and alternate. The round, pink flowers bloom from June through October. Hooked spines arise from the margins of the seedpods.

Habitat/Range: The fragrant mimosa is widespread through our area but is more frequent on limestone. BBNP, CCNP, GMNP.

Comments: Also known as *gatuno* (something that grabs).

Fragrant mimosa.

New Mexico locust.

GEORGE O. MILLER

NEW MEXICO LOCUST
Robinia neomexicana
Legume Family (Fabaceae)

Description: New Mexico locust is best identified by long thorns and compound leaves with rounded leaflets. From May to July large, showy rose-pink flowers grow in clusters at the ends of branches.

Habitat/Range: This attractive legume is found most often at lower elevations in the Guadalupes, especially in canyon bottoms where there is limestone. It is not known to occur elsewhere in the Trans-Pecos region. CCNP, GMNP.

Comments: Deer eat the foliage, while a wide variety of birds and other mammals feed on the seeds.

KATHY ADAMS CLARK

Mescal bean.

MESCAL BEAN
Sophora secundiflora
Legume Family (Fabaceae)

Description: This evergreen plant can grow into a large shrub more than 6 1/2' (2 m) tall. The plants have shiny green, compound leaves throughout the year. From March to May beautiful purple, grape-scented flowers cover the plants, but on any individual they last only a short time. The constricted whitish seedpods contain hard, bright red seeds reportedly toxic to humans.

Habitat/Range: It occurs throughout the lower elevations in the northern Chihuahuan Desert. BBNP, CCNP, FDHS, GMNP.

Comments: With its evergreen foliage and showy flowers, this plant makes an excellent choice for native landscaping. Also known as Texas mountain laurel or *frijolita*.

TEXAS FILAREE
Erodium texanum
Geranium Family (Geraniaceae)

Description: From February to July, Texas filaree blooms with pink-violet to purple flowers with bright yellow anthers. The flowers, with broad petals nearly 1" (2.5 cm) across, usually do not open until late afternoon. As with other native geraniums, filaree has a long style that becomes elastic when mature. This style changes shape as the humidity changes, causing the fruit ("seed") to flop about until it lodges somewhere. The leaves are opposite with rounded lobes.

Habitat/Range: This low-growing annual occurs at lower elevations up to about 4429' (1,350 m). BBNP, CCNP, GMNP.

Comments: Also known as alfilaria.

JEAN HARDY

Texas filaree.

Mexican buckeye.

GEORGE O. MILLER

MEXICAN BUCKEYE
Ungnadia speciosa
Soapberry Family (Sapindaceae)

Description: Mexican buckeye grows as a bush or small tree up to 16' (5 m) in height. The leaflets, with rounded teeth, occur in groups of three to seven. Purplish pink, fragrant flowers bloom before the plant leafs out. The stems are covered with small warts. Inside the woody case are three round, blackish, hard seeds.

Habitat/Range: Mexican buckeye is widespread in our area but is restricted to rocky areas, cliff faces, and stream banks. BBNP, CCNP, FDHS, GMNP.

Comments: The hard seeds are reported to be poisonous to livestock in particular, but many animals, including rock squirrels, feed on them. With its attractive flowers, this would make a fine ornamental bush in xeric gardens. Also known as *monilla.*

Narrowleaf globe mallow.

NARROWLEAF GLOBE MALLOW
Sphaeralcea angustifolia
Mallow Family (Malvaceae)

Description: This erect herb rarely grows more than 5' (1.5 m) tall, usually less than 3' (1 m). The stalk is covered with unlobed, toothed, narrow leaves that are folded midway. Flower color varies from salmon to pink to orange-red, and the flowers can bloom from May through November; if rains are sufficient, they can bloom several times during that period.

Habitat/Range: This widespread perennial occurs commonly throughout our area and may be the globe mallow most frequently encountered. BBNP, CCNP, WSNM.

Comments: This species is browsed by deer and occasionally by cattle. Native Americans used the leaves as a cure for sore eyes, giving rise to another local name, sore-eye poppy.

Saltcedar.

BRENT WAUER

SALTCEDAR
Tamarix chinensis
Tamarisk Family (Tamaricaceae)

Description: The small, overlapping leaves resemble those of junipers. The small pink to white flowers occur from May until late fall.

Habitat/Range: Of the various species of *Tamarix* in the Southwest, *T. chinensis* is the common species in our area, lining riverbanks and low areas where even minimal ground water can be secured. BBNP, GMNP, WSNM.

Comments: This exotic plant arouses much controversy and contention in the Southwest. Several species in this genus were originally introduced as ornamentals and windbreaks and later as agents to help retard soil erosion. All those tasks and more were accomplished. Now, across the Southwest, more than a million acres of critical riparian habitat are occupied by monoculture stands of saltcedar. This has re-sulted in the elimination of many species of native plants and animals. Wildlife has little use for saltcedar, compared to native cottonwoods, willow, and other trees, and many animals have vacated areas where it is dominant. A single saltcedar can produce hundreds of thousands of pollen-sized seeds that are scattered easily. It reproduces through these seeds, as well as twigs and roots. Honeybees make use of the blossoms, and doves nest widely in its thickets. Eliminating saltcedar and replacing it with native vegetation would greatly enhance the overall health of riparian areas. Also known as tamarisk. A similar species, *T. aphylla*, athel, also occurs on sandbars and sandy beaches along the Rio Grande floodplain from Candelaria in Presidio County downriver through Big Bend National Park. Its leaves sheathe the stem.

BRENT WAUER

Scarlet gaura.

SCARLET GAURA
Gaura coccinea
Evening Primrose Family (Onagraceae)

Description: Plants grow up to 20" (50 cm) tall. The flowers, growing along the stem, are pale to white in the evening, deepening to darker pink to reddish by morning. The red-tipped stamens are notable, and the flower is very fragrant. While the normal blooming period is April to October, some flowers can persist into December.

Habitat/Range: This perennial can be locally common at lower elevations. BBNP, CCNP, GMNP, WSNM.

Comments: Moths are the primary pollinators.

VELVET-LEAF GAURA
Gaura parviflora
Evening Primrose Family (Onagraceae)

Description: This plant is often overlooked because of the inconspicuous, small, pinkish white flowers hidden among the large green leaves. The plant can be more than 5' (1.5 m) tall.

Habitat/Range: It is generally found in playas, ditches, and moist low spots, or in disturbed areas. BBNP, CCNP, FDHS, GMNP, WSNM.

Comments: Also known as smallflower gaura.

LEWIS EPPLE

Velvet-leaf gaura.

WHITE-EYE PHLOX
Phlox mesoleuca
Phlox Family (Polemoniaceae)

Description: The flowers have distinctive pink or rose-colored petals with white centers, or "eyes," in the throat. It is a low-growing plant, usually less than 8" (20 cm) tall. The flowers bloom from March through June and rarely again after late summer rains.

Habitat/Range: This attractive pink flower is common throughout much of the middle elevations of our area, growing in groups on rocky outcrops, especially in limestone soil. In some populations, such as in the Big Hill area of Walnut Canyon at Carlsbad Caverns National Park, many individuals are mostly white. BBNP, CCNP, FDHS, GMNP.

White-eye phlox.

Marsh centaury.

MARSH CENTAURY
Centaurium calycosum
Gentian Family (Gentianaceae)

Description: Marsh centaury can grow up to 27" (70 cm) in height but is usually shorter. It is a low-branching plant, and the sparse foliage of lance-shaped or elliptical leaves makes the clusters of flowers look even more abundant. The pinkish tubular flowers have five starlike lobes and a white center. Flowers blossom from April to October.

Habitat/Range: This erect annual is usually found in moist areas, especially along streams and springs. BBNP, CCNP, FDHS, GMNP.

Comments: Also known as *rosita* (little rose).

JEAN HARDY

Showy prairie gentian.

SHOWY PRAIRIE GENTIAN
Eustoma grandiflorum
Gentian Family (Gentianaceae)

Description: The flowers of showy prairie gentian appear in various colors—mostly blue, but also white, violet, pink, and yellow—with white centers. They bloom from June to September. Though usually an annual, in some locales it can persist as a perennial for several years. The leaves are opposite and evenly spaced.

Habitat/Range: This species grows in various habitats, but primarily in moist grasslands, fields, and like areas such as along the Rio Grande. BBNP, WSNM.

Comments: Catch-fly gentian is similar but has much smaller flowers and is normally found in gypsum areas along streams. Also known as *lira de San Pedro* (St. Peter's harp).

PALEFLOWER GILIA
Ipomopsis longiflora
Phlox Family (Polemoniaceae)

Description: The long, pale blue to white, trumpet-shaped flowers, their faces like stars, make this gilia easy to identify. Depending on soil moisture, the flowers may bloom from March to October. The leaves are divided into numerous narrow segments. Paleflower gilia can be up to 27" (69 cm) tall.

Habitat/Range: This showy plant is found primarily in dry, sandy areas and grasslands. BBNP, CCNP, GMNP, WSNM.

Comments: Moths are reported to pollinate the flowers at night, and the plant is said to be good browse.

BRENT WAUER

Paleflower gilia.

GYP PHACELIA
Phacelia integrifolia
Waterleaf Family (Hydrophyllaceae)

Description: The leaves are narrowly scalloped or shallowly lobed, cleft most of the way to the midrib. The stems are reddish, and the flowers are purplish lavender or blue-lavender and bloom from March to September. The plant is up to 16" (40 cm) tall but is usually shorter.

Habitat/Range: This phacelia is found primarily in gypsum or limestone areas. BBNP, CCNP, GMNP, WSNM.

Comments: Also known as toothed-leaf scorpionweed.

Gyp phacelia.

NARROW-LEAVED COLDENIA
Tiquilia hispidissima
Borage Family (Boraginaceae)

Description: The plants are woody at the base and form matted growths 16" (40 cm) wide. Tiny, single pink flowers, only about 3/16" (5 mm) long, appear from May through August.

Habitat/Range: This is another species largely endemic to gypsum, including areas on the western side of Guadalupe Mountains National Park, at White Sands National Monument, and at many isolated locations with minimal gyp deposits. BBNP, CCNP, GMNP, WSNM.

Comments: It is often overlooked because it is low growing and inconspicuous.

Narrow-leaved coldenia.

BRENT WAUER

Desert verbena.

DESERT VERBENA
Verbena wrightii
Vervain Family (Verbenaceae)

Description: The flowers are purple to lavender. It has a long flowering period, being among the earliest in February to among the latest in October.

Habitat/Range: Desert verbena often invades disturbed areas and becomes dominant. After an initial population increase, there seem to be fewer plants in succeeding years at a particular site. This ground-hugging species is widespread in our area in gravelly soils, both limestone and igneous. BBNP, CCNP, FDHS, GMNP.

Comments: Bees and moths are its main pollinators. This would make an attractive ornamental if encouraged. Also known as sand verbena.

RIBBED HEDEOMA
Hedeoma costatum
Mint Family (Lamiaceae)

Description: This densely tufted perennial is covered with curved woolly hairs. The strongly scented plant grows about 6" (15 cm) tall. Lavender flowers in clusters of three to five bloom from April through at least June.

Habitat/Range: Ribbed hedeoma occurs in limestone areas throughout western Texas and in the Guadalupes of southeastern New Mexico. BBNP, CCNP, GMNP.

BRENT WAUER

Ribbed hedeoma.

HOARY ROSEMARY-MINT
Poliomintha incana
Mint Family (Lamiaceae)

Description: This species is usually less than 3' (1 m) tall. It is an aromatic shrub covered with a coat of minute, silvery white hairs. The leaves are linear to inversely lance-shaped. From April through June, pale purple to white flowers occur in clusters of one to three.

Habitat/Range: This species is often found in sandy or gypsum areas. CCNP, GMNP, WSNM.

Comments: This plant was used by Native Americans for seasoning foods. It is good browse for deer.

Hoary rosemary-mint.

Mealy sage.

MEALY SAGE
Salvia farinacea
Mint Family (Lamiaceae)

Description: Mealy sage is a perennial herb that grows to about 27" (69 cm) in height. Dark purple to blue flowers appear in clusters, blooming from April to as late as November. The opposite leaves are linear and long.

Habitat/Range: It occurs primarily in limestone areas on open plains and escarpments and in canyons. CCNP, GMNP.

Comments: This species reportedly offers limited forage value.

BRENT WAUER

Rocky Mountain sage.

ROCKY MOUNTAIN SAGE
Salvia reflexa
Mint Family (Lamiaceae)

Description: The corolla is most commonly purplish to blue, sometimes white.

Habitat/Range: Though generally not common, this annual is found throughout our area, mostly in dry soils in various habitats including open plains and gradual slopes at middle to high elevations. BBNP, CCNP, GMNP.

PURPLE GROUNDCHERRY
Quincula lobata
Nightshade Family (Solanaceae)

Description: Many showy dark purple flowers bloom on this low-growing plant. The flowers are round but have the hint of being lobed and star-shaped. The plant begins producing flowers in March and will continue until the first frost. The leaves are elongated with pinnate lobes.

Habitat/Range: Purple groundcherry is often one of the more conspicuous plants in our area, occurring commonly in open areas. BBNP, CCNP, FDHS, GMNP.

Comments: This diffusely branched herb does well during drought.

JEAN HARDY

Purple groundcherry.

SILVERLEAF NIGHTSHADE
Solanum elaeagnifolium
Nightshade Family (Solanaceae)

Description: This species is best identified by the silver-green oblong leaves; the spines on the leaves, fruit, and stems; and the purple flowers with yellow anthers. Silverleaf nightshade produces a green-striped round fruit that turns yellow as it ripens.

Habitat/Range: Silverleaf nightshade can be extremely common in disturbed areas, where it is often one of the major plants to colonize. BBNP, CCNP, FDHS, GMNP, WSNM.

Comments: The fruit is poisonous but is used to curdle milk to produce asadero cheese. When watered, this plant will produce large numbers of very attractive flowers. Also known as *trompillo.*

Silverleaf nightshade.

SNAPDRAGON MAURANDYA
Maurandya antirrhinifolia
Figwort Family (Scrophulariaceae)

Description: The triangular leaves and five-lobed lavender flowers with a yellow center readily identify this plant. The hairy constriction in the center of the throat of the flower also differentiates it from balloon-sepal maurandya *(Maurandya wislizenii).* The blooming period starts in April and lasts through October if summer rains are sufficient.

Habitat/Range: This is a low-growing or prostrate vine that is often overlooked. It grows over rocks, on cliff faces, or among other plants. This species is normally found at higher elevations than is balloon-sepal maurandya. BBNP, CCNP, FDHS, GMNP.

Snapdragon maurandya.

BRENT WAUER

Downy paintbrush.

DOWNY PAINTBRUSH
Castilleja sessiliflora
Figwort Family (Scrophulariaceae)

Description: This hairy perennial herb has clusters of stems. The flowers are yellow-green, and the petal-like bracts are pinkish with purple veins. It blooms from March to September, occasionally as late as October.

Habitat/Range: Downy paintbrush occurs most frequently in dry, open areas, either sandy or rocky, and usually on limestone soils. It is generally not common. CCNP, GMNP.

BIG BEND SILVERLEAF
Leucophyllum minus
Figwort Family (Scrophulariaceae)

Description: The alternate common name, *cenizo* (ashes), refers to the ashy color of the leaves caused by numerous woolly hairs. This is a many-branched low shrub that can grow up to 3' (1 m) tall. The small lavender to purple flowers, in bloom from June to as late as November, are usually less than 4" (10 cm) across. The leaves are also about that size.

Habitat/Range: Big Bend silverleaf occurs throughout our area at lower elevations in limestone areas and rocky flats. BBNP, CCNP, GMNP.

Comments: This is an important browse plant for deer. Although this is the species most widespread in our area, two other species occur in the southern Trans-Pecos area. One is described; the other, *Leucophyllum candidum*, has leaves that are about as wide as they are long and also has a deep violet flower. It is found only in Brewster County, Texas.

BRENT WAUER

Big Bend silverleaf.

Ceniza.

RICK LOBELLO

CENIZA
Leucophyllum frutescens
Figwort Family (Scrophulariaceae)

Description: The pinkish lavender to white flowers usually last only a short time following rains. This characteristic has inspired another common name, barometer bush. The grayish leaves form a thick mat over the plant, which is usually less than 6' (1.8 m) tall. Depending on rainfall, it can bloom throughout the year but most frequently from June to October.

Habitat/Range: In the wild, ceniza is a limited species growing mostly in limestone areas across the southern parts of Brewster County, including large parts of Big Bend National Park. It is also planted as an ornamental across much of western Texas and into southern New Mexico. BBNP.

Comments: Sheep are reported to browse this species. Also known as purple sage or Texas silverleaf.

COOKIE BALLOU

Fendler's penstemon.

FENDLER'S PENSTEMON

Penstemon fendleri
Figwort Family (Scrophulariaceae)

Description: Fendler's penstemon has many slender, bluish purple to lavender flowers that grow in whorls around the stem. The flowers have purple lines in the throat on the lower lip, and golden hairs are visible in the throat of the corolla. The flowers bloom from April to August. This is a short perennial, generally no more than 16" (40 cm) tall. The leaves are triangular and folded.

Habitat/Range: This species is found in open areas in both sandy and rocky soil. BBNP, CCNP, FDHS, GMNP.

DESERT WILLOW

Chilopsis linearis
Catalpa Family (Bignoniaceae)

Description: Although the long, narrow leaves resemble those of some willows, this is not a true willow. It occurs as a shrub or a tree and can be as tall as 33' (10 m). Trunks are generally not straight but leaning. The large flower is highly variable in color, ranging from white, to purplish red, to pinkish white, the predominant color in most areas. Desert willow generally blooms in May and June but occasionally at other times of the year after a heavy rain. Irrigated trees flower throughout the summer and early fall. The long, narrow fruits are also distinctive.

Habitat/Range: It generally occurs along streams, riversides, and in dry canyons. BBNP, CCNP, FDHS, GMNP, WSNM.

Comments: Desert willow is important as a nesting site for birds, and the flowers are an important food source for hummingbirds and insects. Native Americans wove baskets from the twigs. Also known as *mimbre* (wicker).

C. ALLAN MORGAN

Desert willow.

NPS PHOTO

Shaggy stenandrium.

SHAGGY STENANDRIUM
Stenandrium barbatum
Acanthus Family (Acanthaceae)

Description: This low-growing perennial is often overlooked except when the 3/8" (1 cm) reddish pink flower draws attention to the plant. This species blooms in the spring, most frequently in April and May but occasionally in March and as late as early September. The two-lipped flower is streaked with white toward the base.

Habitat/Range: It is found in dry limestone soils, often with stands of lechuguilla. BBNP, CCNP, GMNP.

Comments: Also known as shaggy tuft.

BRENT WAUER

Bluebells.

BLUEBELLS
Campanula rotundifolia
Bluebell Family (Campanulaceae)

Description: This perennial is easily identified by the presence of the blue to violet-blue drooping flowers on an erect stem that is up to 17" (43 cm) tall. The plant has round to elliptical basal leaves but has linear leaves along the stem of the plant. The flowering period is from at least June through September and sometimes into October.

Habitat/Range: Bluebells are found largely in moist lowland areas, but they can occur at higher elevations also. BBNP, CCNP, GMNP.

SISKIYOU ASTER
Aster hesperius
Sunflower Family (Asteraceae)

Description: Clumps of this plant are formed by rhizomes. The flowers range from white to light pink to light blue. This is one of the fall composites, with flowers blooming from August to November.

Habitat/Range: Siskiyou aster is a slender perennial most frequently found along streams and similar moist areas, usually above 3281' (1000 m) elevation. BBNP, GMNP.

Siskiyou aster.

Basketflower.

BASKETFLOWER
Centaurea americana
Sunflower Family (Asteraceae)

Description: This tall annual often approaches 5' (1.5 m) in height. The lance-shaped leaves clasp the stems. From April to July a large, wide flower, up to 4" (10 cm) across, tops the stem. The odd-looking bloom lacks ray flowers; the disk flowers have a light pink to white center rimmed with lavender.

Habitat/Range: Basketflower often grows in groups, especially in caliche-rich areas, areas with a calcium carbonate crust on the soil. BBNP, CCNP, GMNP, WSNM.

Comments: Also known as *tacalote*.

BRENT WAUER

Wright thoroughwort.

WRIGHT THOROUGHWORT
Eupatorium wrightii
Sunflower Family (Asteraceae)

Description: This shrubby plant is up to 27" (69 cm) tall. The leaves are opposite, small, triangular, and up to 3/4" (2 cm) long. The plant produces purple flowers from August through mid-November.

Habitat/Range: This species is found from 3445' to 6070' (1050 m to 1850 m) in elevation. It is found mainly in limestone areas, but in the Chisos Mountains it is found in igneous areas. BBNP, CCNP, GMNP.

Comments: This plant is sometimes listed in the genus *Ageratina*. Also known as oregano.

BLAZING STAR
Liatris punctata
Sunflower Family (Asteraceae)

Description: Blazing star, a perennial, can grow up to 27" (69 cm) tall but is usually shorter. The long stalks of pink to purple feathery ray flowers make this a very attractive plant.

Habitat/Range: This species occurs across much of western North America but is nowhere common. It is most frequently found on canyon slopes and shortgrass prairies, especially in areas with caliche, a calcium carbonate crust on the soil. BBNP, CCNP, FDHS, GMNP.

Comments: When stressed for food, Native Americans cooked and ate the roots. Also known as dotted gayfeather.

WALT SHIPLEY

Blazing star.

Texas skeleton plant.

BRENT WAUER

TEXAS SKELETON PLANT
Lygodesmia texana
Sunflower Family (Asteraceae)

Description: This slender, stalked plant with grasslike leaves can be up to 16" (40 cm) tall. Rose-lavender ray flowers bloom from April through late October. The petals fall easily from the delicate flowers. A milky substance seeps out when the stems or leaves are broken.

Habitat/Range: This perennial can be locally common in open grasslands and rocky hillsides. CCNP, FDHS, GMNP.

Comments: Native Americans chewed the coagulated milky sap and boiled the leaves of the plant with meat.

JEAN HARDY

Tahoka daisy.

TAHOKA DAISY
Machaeranthera tanacetifolia
Sunflower Family (Asteraceae)

Description: Fernlike leaves and yellow disk and purplish ray flowers help to identify this plant. This annual, up to 1' (30 cm) tall, blooms from June through October.

Habitat/Range: This widespread composite is likely to be found anywhere at lower elevations in open areas with compact and sandy soils. It is, however, often very common along roadsides and disturbed places. BBNP, CCNP, GMNP, WSNM.

Comments: Also known as tansyleaf spine aster.

GREEN AND/OR TINY FLOWERS

*This section includes green flowers and
the tiny, non-showy, and/or unisexual flowers of
some of the tree species.*

Havard wild buckwheat.

HAVARD WILD BUCKWHEAT
Eriogonum havardii
Knotweed Family (Polygonaceae)

Description: The plant is largely low grow-ing with a base of gray, oblong leaves. From June to October, small yellow flowers only about 1/4" (0.5 cm) across appear at the end of a slender stalk that can be up to 2' (60 cm) tall.

Habitat/Range: This fairly widespread buck-wheat is most often encountered in rocky, es-pecially limestone, soils. CCNP, GMNP.

ROUNDLEAF WILD BUCKWHEAT
Eriogonum rotundifolium
Knotweed Family (Polygonaceae)

Description: The plant is up to 15" (38 cm) tall. The bright green basal leaves last only a brief time, leaving largely naked stems. Many white flowers occur from March through early November.

Habitat/Range: This is a widespread annual throughout our area, occurring mostly at lower elevations areas in sandy or gravelly soil. GMNP, WSNM.

Roundleaf wild buckwheat.

DESERT RHUBARB
Rumex hymenosepalus
Knotweed Family (Polygonaceae)

Description: The plant grows to more than 3' (1 m) high, with an upright base of large, oblong leaves up to 1' (30 cm) long. The abundant red-brown seeds crowd the stalk. The plant grows from a group of large roots. Tiny pink flowers along the stalk are present from as early as February through May.

Habitat/Range: Desert rhubarb, also known as pale dock or canigre, is mostly limited in our area to sandy sites. CCNP, FDHS, GMNP.

Comments: The tubers are rich in tannin and were used in the tanning industry. Because of their strong alumlike quality, the tubers were also chewed to tighten gums.

GEORGE O. MILLER

Desert rhubarb.

BRENT WAUER

Mountain mahogany.

MOUNTAIN MAHOGANY
Cercocarpus montanus
Rose Family (Rosaceae)

Description: This shrub is usually 6 1/2' (2 m) tall or less. It is best identified by the simple alternate leaves. The yellow flowers arise either solitarily or in groups of twos or threes. A fuzzy, spiraled awn is attached to each fruit.

Habitat/Range: Common throughout much of the higher portions of our area, typically growing in thick stands on canyon sides and ridgetops. BBNP, CCNP, GMNP.

Comments: Mountain mahogany withstands grazing and is readily eaten by deer and elk. It is helpful in preventing erosion. Also known as *lintisco*.

LEWIS EPPLE

Rock mat.

ROCK MAT
Petrophytum caespitosum
Rose Family (Rosaceae)

Description: Large colonies of this plant spill over sloping rock faces, and the leaves are so tightly compact the plant itself resembles a smooth gray-green stone. From June through September it bears dense growths of small white flowers.

Habitat/Range: Because of its low-growing, rock-clinging habit, rock mat is often overlooked. It occurs throughout western Texas and southern New Mexico. BBNP, CCNP, GMNP.

Comments: Also known as tufted rock mat.

SKUNKBUSH
Ptelea trifoliata
Citrus Family (Rutaceae)

Description: This plant can grow up to 20' (6 m) tall. The thin, deciduous leaves are three-parted and up to 10" (25 cm) in length. Leaves are alternate or opposite, and the marks they leave on the stem are U-shaped. The small, pale yellow to greenish white flowers bloom from April through July. The circular, flat, waferlike fruits are paperlike in texture and contain two seeds.

Habitat/Range: This wide-ranging small tree or shrub occurs throughout our area at higher elevations. BBNP, CCNP, GMNP.

Comments: When the leaves and twigs are crushed, they give off a musty odor, hence the common name skunkbush. Also known as common hoptree.

BRENT WAUER

Skunkbush.

NEW MEXICO CROTON
Croton dioicus
Spurge Family (Euphorbiaceae)

Description: This species can reach heights of 27" (69 cm), but it is usually much shorter. It is often woody at the base and bears many silvery leaves. Inconspicuous male and female flowers occur on separate plants.

Habitat/Range: This perennial herb can be very common in the northern Chihuahuan Desert in sandy and rocky areas. New Mexico croton is one of the more common species of the genus, especially in heavily grazed areas, although several others occur in our area, too. BBNP, CCNP, GMNP, WSNM.

Comments: Deer occasionally browse this plant, and doves feed on the seeds. Also known as grassland croton.

New Mexico croton.

Rattlesnake weed.

RATTLESNAKE WEED
Euphorbia albomarginata
Spurge Family (Euphorbiaceae)

Description: The small, opposite leaves are mostly oblong, but they can be round or long, with narrow white margins and a red speck in the center of most leaves. When broken, the stems exude a milky sap. Many small white flowers often cover the plant from April to November.

Habitat/Range: This plant hugs the ground in thin mats and is locally common in our area, on open clay and limestone soils. BBNP, CCNP, GMNP, WSNM.

Comments: As the common name suggests, rattlesnake weed was once thought useful in treating snakebites. Another common name is white-margin spurge.

GEORGE O. MILLER

Allthorn.

ALLTHORN
Koeberlinia spinosa
Allthorn Family (Koeberliniaceae)

Description: This many-branched shrub is usually leafless and carries out much of its photosynthesis through the thorns and twigs. It rarely attains heights greater than 16' (5 m). Its small, greenish white flowers bloom from May to October, followed by reddish to black berries that are eaten by many birds and mammals.

Habitat/Range: Although widespread, allthorn is limited in distribution and generally not common in our area. It is often found only in scattered sites at lower elevations. BBNP, CCNP, FDHS, GMNP, WSNM.

Comments: Allthorn serves as a nesting site and refuge for many species of animals. It seems to be in decline, with the generation of young plants rare in much of the northern Chihuahuan Desert. Also known as crucifixion thorn or *junco*.

SEA-LAVENDER
Limonium limbatum
Plumbago Family (Plumbaginaceae)

Description: Healthy sea-lavender has broad basal leaves topped with very small lavender flowers. It blooms from June through August.

Habitat/Range: In our area sea-lavender occurs in low saline areas in White Sands National Monument. Outside park areas, many populations of this plant have declined severely due to pollutants dumped in playas. WSNM.

Comments: Its presence is a good indicator of a healthy playa.

D. VASQUEZ

Sea-lavender.

BRENT WAUER

Longhorn milkweed.

LONGHORN MILKWEED
Asclepias oenotheroides
Milkweed Family (Asclepiadaceae)

Description: This is a low-growing perennial herb, only about 1' (0.3 m) in height. The common name comes from the conspicuously stalked horns on the greenish flowers, which bloom from June to September. As with other milkweeds, the plant produces milky sap and silky plumed seeds that are dispersed by the wind. The plant usually is covered with oval to oblong leaves.

Habitat/Range: Longhorn milkweed is a dryland plant found in a wide variety of soils, often in limestone grassland, at low to middle elevations. BBNP, CCNP, FDHS, GMNP.

Comments: Also known as *hierba de zizotes*.

BRENT WAUER

Green-flower puccoon.

GREEN-FLOWER PUCCOON
Lithospermum viride
Borage Family (Boraginaceae)

Description: This perennial has a woody tap-root and grows up to 3' (1 m) tall. The number of stems can vary from only a few to many. The largest leaves occur at the middle of the stem. Clusters of tubular, greenish yellow flowers bloom from May to September, occasionally October.

Habitat/Range: Green-flower puccoon is found on both limestone and igneous soils. BBNP, CCNP, GMNP.

Comments: Some authors report that Native Americans obtained a purple dye from the roots.

DESERT TOBACCO
Nicotiana trigonophylla
Nightshade Family (Solanaceae)

Description: This is a short, stout herb less than 3' (1 m) tall, with few branches. The trumpet-shaped, sticky, greenish white flowers occur in loose clusters from March through November. The oval leaves clasp the stem.

Habitat/Range: This is a native tobacco that is uncommon in the area. It grows in a wide variety of lowland habitats including sandy washes and protected places on cliff faces. BBNP, CCNP, GMNP.

BRENT WAUER

Desert tobacco.

BRENT WAUER

Heartleaf groundcherry.

HEARTLEAF GROUNDCHERRY
Physalis hederaefolia
Nightshade Family (Solanaceae)

Description: The leaves, broad but short with wavy margins, are dark green with a few gray hairs. The flowers are yellow to greenish yellow with solid black spots at the base of the petals and bright yellow anthers. The plant blooms from April through September and grows up to 19" (48 cm) tall.

Habitat/Range: This low-growing perennial herb is most often found in dry areas, such as plains and sandy areas. BBNP, CCNP, FDHS, GMNP.

LEWIS EPPLE

English plantain.

ENGLISH PLANTAIN
Plantago lanceolata
Plantain Family (Plantaginaceae)

Description: This Old World introduction is likely to be the plantain that people first notice. It is best identified by the basal cluster of long lance-shaped leaves. English plantain is taller than desert plantain, ranging up to 35" (89 cm). Dense brown flower spikes top the stem. It has been recorded blooming from April to August and frequently longer.

Habitat/Range: It grows at low elevations and does well in disturbed areas. CCNP, GMNP.

Comments: Also known as buckhorn.

DWARF PRAIRIE CONEFLOWER
Ratibida tagetes
Sunflower Family (Asteraceae)

Description: This is a bushy composite up to 16" (40 cm) tall with many short, stalked heads. Leaves are pinnate with linear leaflets. The flower consists of a spherical disk covered with maroon disk flowers. Five to seven yellow ray flowers, which are spotted with yellow to reddish brown, surround the base of the disk flowers. Dwarf prairie coneflower blooms from June to September.

Habitat/Range: This short coneflower occurs in dry areas, usually with little slope, and is often locally common to abundant. CCNP, GMNP.

MARK PETERSON

Dwarf prairie coneflower.

BLUE FLOWERS

*Bluish flowers often grade into
other hues, so you should also check
the pink and purple flower section.*

BRENT WAUER

Erect dayflower.

ERECT DAYFLOWER
Commelina erecta
Spiderwort Family (Commelinaceae)

Description: Large, bright blue side petals bring attention to dayflower, as it starts to bloom in May, continuing through much of the summer with sufficient moisture.

Habitat/Range: This common prostrate plant is usually overlooked unless it is in bloom. BBNP, CCNP, GMNP.

Comments: Flowers often last for only a day or less. Erect dayflower seems to prefer moist, rocky areas. Known as *hierba de pollo* (chicken weed) in Spanish.

BIG BEND BLUEBONNET
Lupinus havardii
Legume Family (Fabaceae)

Description: Within the blue flower is a creamy-white square covered with many dark yellow spots that turn red as the flower ages. Occasionally white "bluebonnets" are found. Plants can bloom as early as January and occasionally into June if moisture is sufficient. The plant reaches a height of 32" (81 cm).

Habitat/Range: A trip to Big Bend National Park during a good bluebonnet year will provide a memory of a lifetime. With its profusion of purple-blue flowers during certain springtimes, the Big Bend bluebonnet is a remarkable plant. It is the only bluebonnet found in the northern Chihuahuan Desert. It prefers rocky areas and is frequently abundant along roadsides and often grows in association with lechuguilla. BBNP.

Comments: Deer reportedly browse on young plants.

Big Bend bluebonnet.

Prairie flax.

PRAIRIE FLAX
Linum lewisii
Flax Family (Linaceae)

Description: A perennial, prairie flax can grow up to 27" (69 cm) tall, with leafy stems. Delicate sky blue flowers bloom from May through August, and the petals drop easily if handled.

Habitat/Range: This widespread flax occurs from Alaska to northern Mexico, and in our area it is found in a wide variety of habitats from dry, sandy, or rocky hills to coniferous forests. BBNP, CCNP, GMNP.

Comments: In some parts of New Mexico the seeds are ground and mixed with cornmeal to treat infections and diminish swelling. Also known as blue prairie flax.

NPS PHOTO

Blue morning glory.

BLUE MORNING GLORY
Ipomoea lindheimeri
Morning Glory Family (Convolvulaceae)

Description: This is an herbaceous vine with deeply cleft leaves that often drapes over other bushes or rock piles. The funnel-shaped bluish purple flowers, up to 3" (8 cm) across, are present from July to October.

Habitat/Range: Blue morning glory is restricted to sandy and rocky areas where it can be locally common. BBNP, CCNP, FDHS, GMNP.

Comments: Many animals browse this plant.

Canyon sage.

BRENT WAUER

CANYON SAGE
Salvia lycioides
Mint Family (Lamiaceae)

Description: A small cluster of blue flowers is present from April to October, sometimes into November. A perennial, woody, stemmed shrub, it reaches up to 19" (48 cm) high.

Habitat/Range: Canyon sage is a widespread species at higher elevations in our area in canyons, on rocky slopes, and occasionally on ledges. It is most frequently found at elevations above 5249' (1600 m) in the Guadalupe Mountains. BBNP, CCNP, GMNP.

ORANGE AND RED FLOWERS

This section includes red and orange flowers, as well as those with a maroon or brownish cast. Since red flowers grade into pink and purple flowers, readers looking for red flowers should check the pink and purple, and blue sections as well.

SCARLET MUSK-FLOWER
Nyctaginia capitata
Four-O'Clock Family (Nyctaginaceae)

Description: Scarlet musk-flower is an attractive plant, growing low to the ground often along roadsides and covered with stunning, bright red flowers with long, extended stamens. Blooms occur from April to as late as September depending on adequate moisture.

Habitat/Range: This widespread but uncommon plant occurs most frequently in loamy or sandy soil. BBNP, CCNP, FDHS, GMNP.

Comments: The scent earns it the name "musk-flower." Also known as devil's bouquet.

BRENT WAUER

Scarlet musk-flower.

SHAGGY PORTULACA
Portulaca mundula
Purslane Family (Portulacaceae)

Description: This herbaceous annual has alternate, succulent leaves, with plant hairs rising from the leaf axils. The round leaves are up to ⅝" (1.5 cm) long and just as wide. When water is available, the reddish purple flowers bloom from spring through late summer.

Habitat/Range: BBNP, CCNP, GMNP, WSNM.

Comments: Shaggy portulaca grows from a taproot, usually in a prostrate or slightly ascending form. The plant was used extensively by Native Americans as food and as treatment for urinary problems. Also known as *chisma*.

G. STOLZ

Shaggy portulaca.

Mexican catch-fly.

MEXICAN CATCH-FLY
Silene laciniata
Pink Family (Caryophyllaceae)

Description: Occasionally reaching 23" (59 cm) in height, most plants are closer to 1' (30 cm). The stems are hairy. It is easily identified when in bloom because of the brilliant scarlet tubular flowers. The flowers are up to 1 ½" (4 cm) in diameter, and each of the five petals are sliced at the tip into four sharp points. The stamens have green anthers. The blooming period lasts from May to October. Also known as Mexican campion.

Habitat/Range: This is one of the more attractive perennials found in our area. It grows in the mountains, generally above 4429' (1350 m), often in the shade of an oak or madrone tree. BBNP, CCNP, GMNP.

Comments: Insects are occasionally caught in the sticky bands between the upper leaves, hence the name catch-fly.

DESERT ROSE
Rosa stellata
Rose Family (Rosaceae)

Description: Desert rose reaches a height of 3' (1 m) or more. The leaves are pinnately compound, and the stems are covered with small, yellowish prickles. From June to as late as September, flowers bloom at the terminal end of the branches. The flowers are rose-purple and though usually solitary may occur in small clusters.

Habitat/Range: Desert rose occurs infrequently in our area, rarely at low elevations to middle-level sites around 6562' (2000 m). This shrub is found in dry, well-drained rocky places, preferably on limestone. CCNP, GMNP.

Desert rose.

RANGE RATANY
Krameria glandulosa
Ratany Family (Krameraceae)

Description: Generally a low shrub, 27" (70 cm) or less in height, it has many branches covered with scattered, alternate leaves. Flowers first appear in April and may persist through the summer.

Habitat/Range: Range ratany is often locally common in our area in rocky locations up to 4987' (1520 m) in elevation. BBNP, CCNP, GMNP.

GEORGE O. MILLER

Range ratany.

BOWL FLAX
Linum berlandieri
Flax Family (Linaceae)

Description: Bowl flax is easy to recognize when in bloom. Its bright yellow or copper flowers have a dark reddish center with yellow anthers. The plant continues to produce blossoms from April to September. The leaves are narrow. The plant grows up to 16" (40 cm) in height depending on local conditions.

Habitat/Range: This annual of the prairies is uncommon here, found in open flat areas, though sometimes in rocky soil, too. BBNP, CCNP, GMNP.

Comments: Also known as Berlandier flax.

BRENT WAUER

Bowl flax.

BRENT WAUER

Soft orange globe mallow.

SOFT ORANGE GLOBE MALLOW
Sphaeralcea incana
Mallow Family (Malvaceae)

Description: This plant can be more than 3' (1 m) in height. The leaves are only shallowly lobed. The flowers range from red to pink and bloom between June and October.

Habitat/Range: This globe mallow can be a locally abundant perennial in our area. It prefers deep, sandy soil, but it is also found in grassy areas with rocky soils. CCNP, GMNP, WSNM.

Comments: This plant is browsed by deer and, to a lesser extent, by livestock. As with all species in this genus, absolute identification can only be made by examining the patterns of veins on the walls of sections of the fruit, which look like tiny wedges of cheese.

WRINKLED GLOBE MALLOW
Sphaeralcea subhastata
Mallow Family (Malvaceae)

Description: The green leaf blades are arrow-shaped and have short side lobes. Clusters of stems form dense leafy clumps. The flowers are grenadine to pink, blooming from March to October, occasionally as late as November.

Habitat/Range: This perennial is found in open areas, along roadsides, and in grasslands, often where limestone and limestone soils occur. BBNP, CCNP, WSNM.

Comments: As with the other globe mallows, this species is browsed by deer and livestock.

BRENT WAUER

Wrinkled globe mallow.

BEARDLIP PENSTEMON
Penstemon barbatus
Figwort Family (Scrophulariaceae)

Description: This widespread perennial penstemon is an upright plant that grows up to 3' (1 m) tall. The slender bright scarlet flower has a broad face, and the lower lip bends back while the top lip projects forward. The lower lip usually bears a few yellow hairs. The flowers, which occur in loose clusters, droop slightly downward. They bloom from June to September, occasionally as late as October. Dark green leaves and stout stems also mark this species of the dry pine-oak woodlands.

Habitat/Range: BBNP, CCNP, FDHS, GMNP.

Comments: Also known as *jarritos* (small pitchers).

Beardlip penstemon.

Cardinal penstemon.

CARDINAL PENSTEMON
Penstemon cardinalis
Figwort Family (Scrophulariaceae)

Description: Cardinal penstemon is best identified by the large heart-shaped leaves and cardinal red flowers that are constricted at the entrance. The flowers bloom from May to August. This perennial herb occurs as single plants or in small groups.

Habitat/Range: Cardinal penstemon is an attractive wildflower of the Guadalupe Mountains. It is partial to limestone areas, often being most common at the base and lower face of limestone cliffs. Although generally not uncommon in its preferred habitat, its limited geographic range has led to its being listed in New Mexico as a rare and sensitive species. CCNP, GMNP.

Comments: Also known as Guadalupe penstemon.

BRENT WAUER

Arizona honeysuckle.

ARIZONA HONEYSUCKLE
Lonicera arizonica
Honeysuckle Family (Caprifoliaceae)

Description: This species is similar to western white honeysuckle but has red flowers (orange on the inside) and hairy leaves.

Habitat/Range: This species generally grows at higher elevations, above 5906' (1800 m). It is not frequently encountered and is known in our area only the Guadalupe Mountains. CCNP, GMNP.

Comments: Also known as *madreselva* (mother of the forest).

SLIMLOBE GLOBEBERRY
Ibervillea tenuisecta
Gourd Family (Cucurbitaceae)

Description: The leaves are deeply divided into slender lobes, and the unripe fruit resembles a small, round green watermelon about the size of a marble. The bright red ripe fruit closely resembles a cherry tomato, but it is probably not edible.

Habitat/Range: Globeberry is often overlooked because it usually grows within another plant, especially one with thorns such as mesquite or allthorn. These serve as "foster" plants, among which the long, slender vine of the globeberry can grow. BBNP, CCNP, FDHS, GMNP.

GEORGE O. MILLER

Slimlobe globeberry.

BRENT WAUER

Cardinal flower.

CARDINAL FLOWER
Lobelia cardinalis
Bluebell Family (Campanulaceae)

Description: Brilliant dark red flowers draw instant attention to this plant and provide an obvious feature for identification. The flowering period is long, from May to at least October and occasionally December. Lance-shaped leaves occur on the plant, which reaches up to 6 ½' (2 m) in height.

Habitat/Range: Cardinal flower grows in damp soil and shady areas. BBNP, CCNP, GMNP.

Comments: This is an important species for deer, which use it for browse, and for hummingbirds and sulphur butterflies, which feed on the nectar and pollinate the flowers.

BRENT WAUER

Wavyleaf thistle.

WAVYLEAF THISTLE
Cirsium undulatum
Sunflower Family (Asteraceae)

Description: Wavyleaf thistle is a tall perennial that reaches up to 6 ½' (2 m) in height. The prickly leaves are covered with a thick growth of tangled whitish hairs. The flower heads are terminal and stout. The flower heads vary in color from lavender to purple to almost white, all bleaching to white as they age. Flowers appear by early May and persist through most of the summer. This common thistle grows singly or in groups.

Habitat/Range: This is one of many thistles one is likely to encounter in our area and throughout the West. BBNP, CCNP, FDHS, GMNP.

Comments: Deer browse young thistles before the prickles make this difficult, and goldfinches line their nests with thistle down in mid- to late summer.

JEAN HARDY

Firewheel.

FIREWHEEL
Gaillardia pulchella
Sunflower Family (Asteraceae)

Description: The plant is usually less than 1' (30 cm) tall, with flowers that are about 4" (10 cm) across. The three-lobed ray flowers are purple at the base, gradually changing to yellow at the tips. The disk flowers in the center are light purple to red. The plant blooms from March through October.

Habitat/Range: This annual herb occurs throughout our area, generally at lower elevations and in areas with sandy soil. GMNP.

Comments: Also known as Indian blanket, this plant tolerates heat and dryness well.

YELLOW FLOWERS

This section includes flowers ranging from bright golden yellow and yellow-orange to pale, creamy yellow. Since yellow flowers grade into red, pink, and white flowers, readers looking for yellow flowers should check the orange and red, pink and purple, and white sections as well.

COPPER ZEPHYRLILY
Zephryanthus longifolia
Amaryllis Family (Amaryllidaceae)

Description: This beautiful plant has showy yellow flowers that are over 1" (2.5 m) across; the leaves are few. This plant grows from a bulb and blooms for a long time, from April to August, depending on adequate rainfall. Flowering may be limited during drought.

Habitat/Range: Copper zephyrlily occurs in igneous and limestone soils, especially where gravel predominates. CCNP.

Copper zephyrlily.

Fleshy tidestromia.

FLESHY TIDESTROMIA
Tidestromia lanuginosa
Amaranth Family (Amaranthaceae)

Description: Minute yellow flowers adorn this ground-hugging plant from March to October. The yellow stems branch repeatedly; this plant is a good ground cover. The leaves are covered with small starlike hairs that disappear as the plant matures.

Habitat/Range: CCNP, GMNP, WSNM.

Comments: Known in Spanish as *espanta vaqueros* (it frightens cattlemen).

NPS PHOTO

LEWIS EPPLE

BRENT WAUER

Guadalupe columbine.

GUADALUPE COLUMBINE
Aquilegia chaplinei
Crowfoot Family (Ranunculaceae)

Description: The plant grows up to 19" (48 cm) in height; the leaves are divided. Pale yellow flowers appear from April to November.

Habitat/Range: This columbine is one of the beautiful surprises you may encounter while hiking in the Guadalupe Mountains. Most often, it grows wherever there is permanent water, but it can also be found in moist places where surface water is not apparent. This species is easily found in McKittrick Canyon in the Guadalupes or in the adjacent Lincoln National Forest at Sitting Bull Falls. CCNP, GMNP.

Comments: Diversion of water from these sites could threaten this locally common species.

Longspur columbine.

LONGSPUR COLUMBINE

Aquilegia longissima
Crowfoot Family (Ranunculaceae)

Description: The flowers have the typical columbine shape, except that the spurs are very long, up to 7" (20 cm) in length. The petals are dark yellow, and the flowers bloom from June to October. The light yellow-green leaves have three lobes. The plant grows up to 3' (1 m) in height.

Habitat/Range: This columbine is restricted to the Chisos Mountains in Big Bend National Park and adjacent northeastern Mexico. Longspur columbine is found where there is dripping water and at other moist places in mountain canyons. BBNP.

Comments: Because this species occurs in areas of high visitor use, the numbers of this very limited plant have dramatically declined because of collecting of flowers and disturbance.

BRENT WAUER

Red barberry.

RED BARBERRY
Berberis haematocarpa
Barberry Family (Berberidaceae)

Description: This barberry is easily distinguished from others by its shrubby growth, five to seven spine-tipped teeth on the leaves, and the overall darker green color of the leaves, which are alternate. It grows as much as 6 ½' (2 m) tall. Bright yellow flowers occur from February through April, and the plant produces showy red berries. The stems have a bright yellow inner bark.

Habitat/Range: Red barberry can be found in mountains and desert canyons, at slightly higher elevations than algerita, from 4593' (1400 m) to 7218' (2200 m). BBNP, CCNP, GMNP.

CREEPING BARBERRY
Berberis repens
Barberry Family (Berberidaceae)

Description: Although the leaves are broader than other species of *Berberis*, they are still stiff and prickly. Fragrant yellow flowers are produced from March through June.

Habitat/Range: Creeping barberry is found in forested canyons at higher elevations. It is low growing or barely climbs onto rocks or other plants, making a good ground cover. CCNP, GMNP.

Comments: As with the other species, a jelly can be made from the fruit. Also known as Oregon grape.

BRENT WAUER

Creeping barberry.

ALGERITA
Berberis trifoliolata
Barberry Family (Berberidaceae)

Description: Algerita grows as tall as 6 ½' (2 m) and is covered with alternate, spiny three-part leaflets. Bright yellow flowers occur as early as February, although some plants may not bloom until April.

Habitat/Range: This common shrub is found throughout much of our area, often forming thickets at lower elevations. BBNP, CCNP, FDHS, GMNP.

Comments: The extremely fragrant, pleasing flowers cover most of the plant, but they last only a few days. When the fruits ripen in May and June, they are quickly eaten by birds and small mammals. Native Americans obtained a yellow dye from the stems of plants of this genus, and the roots have been used for everything from a remedy for toothache to curing deer hides.

RICK LOBELLO

Algerita.

LEWIS EPPLE

Western wall-flower.

WESTERN WALL-FLOWER
Erysimum capitatum
Mustard Family (Brassicaceae)

Description: The plant grows up to 3' (1 m) high and is composed of erect stems that may or may not be branched in the upper half. The flowers range in color from orange to yellow. This perennial blooms from early February to as late as September.

Habitat/Range: This widespread species occurs in our area more frequently at higher elevations. It prefers rocky areas. BBNP, CCNP, GMNP.

Fendler's bladder pod.

FENDLER'S BLADDER POD
Lesquerella fendleri
Mustard Family (Brassicaceae)

Description: The four-petaled flowers are handsome against the distinctly silvery foliage. The plant's color is due to the abundance of minute, dense, starlike silver hairs that cover the entire surface of the plant. Its mostly erect stems, reaching to 6" (15 cm) tall, bear narrow leaves, a few of which are usually toothed. Often abundant, it is one of the earliest plants to bloom, starting in January and continuing through April, covering tracts of land with bright yellow flowers.

Habitat/Range: This small mustard occurs in rocky or sandy soil, especially where there is gypsum, at lower elevations throughout the northern Chihuahuan Desert. BBNP, CCNP, FDHS, GMNP, WSNM.

Comments: The species is occasionally browsed by deer.

WHITETHORN ACACIA
Acacia constricta
Legume Family (Fabaceae)

Description: The branches on this shrub are spreading or straight and are adorned with pairs of slightly curved spines at the nodes. The leaves have four to seven pairs of pinnae. The fragrant yellow flowers bloom from June through August, somewhat earlier than those of viscid acacia, the species it most closely resembles.

Habitat/Range: Whitethorn acacia is one of the more widespread acacias in the northern Chihuahuan Desert, commonly found at lower elevations but ranging up to 6234' (1900 m). BBNP, CCNP, FDHS, GMNP.

Comments: Bees are attracted to whitethorn acacia, and many animals, including quail, feed on the seeds.

Whitethorn acacia.

VISCID ACACIA
Acacia neovernicosa
Legume Family (Fabaceae)

Description: Viscid acacia is similar to whitethorn acacia but can be told apart by its having one to two, occasionally three, pairs of leaflets that look as if they were varnished. This species flowers from April through July.

Habitat/Range: As with other acacias, viscid acacia occurs on gravelly hillsides and produces yellow, fragrant flowers. BBNP, CCNP, GMNP.

Comments: When it and whitethorn acacia occur together, viscid acacia produces flowers about two weeks later.

Viscid acacia.

LINDHEIMER SENNA
Cassia lindheimeriana
Legume Family (Fabaceae)

Description: One to several erect stems, covered with pinnately compound leaves, branch from the base. The oval or elliptical leaflets number five to eight pairs. Plants are usually 3' (1 m) tall, but some attain a height up to 6 ½' (2 m). The golden flowers have oval petals crimped along the edges. Lindheimer senna blooms from June through November.

Habitat/Range: This perennial herb is found commonly on limestone soils throughout the northern Chihuahuan Desert at elevations up to 5577' (1700 m). BBNP, CCNP, FDHS, GMNP, WSNM.

Lindheimer senna.

Wright's dalea.

WRIGHT'S DALEA
Dalea wrightii
Legume Family (Fabaceae)

Description: Wright's dalea is usually less than 5 ½" (14 cm) tall. Five to seven leaf segments are covered with silky hair, and the yellow flowers appear from April to September.

Habitat/Range: Wright's dalea is a low-spreading perennial found most often in gravelly soil and grassland at lower elevations. BBNP, CCNP, GMNP.

Comments: This is generally less common than other daleas.

HOG POTATO
Hoffmanseggia glauca
Legume Family (Fabaceae)

Description: This perennial, which sometimes reaches 1' (30 cm) in height, has many pinnately compound leaves. The small yellow flowers have an upper petal covered with red-orange dots near the base. Blooming occurs from March through September.

Habitat/Range: Although generally common along roads and in other disturbed areas at lower elevations, the hog potato is often overlooked. BBNP, CCNP, FDHS, GMNP, WSNM.

JEAN HARDY

Hog potato.

GEORGE O. MILLER

Honey mesquite.

HONEY MESQUITE
Prosopis glandulosa
Legume Family (Fabaceae)

Description: In warmer climates this species becomes tree-sized, but in our area it is usually a shrub. One individual at Big Bend National Park has attained a height of 42' (12.8 m). Spines, either single or double, cover the branches. Leaves are alternate and bipinnate. From May through late summer spikes of yellow flowers appear. The constricted pods are 4-8" (10-20 cm) long, and in years of good moisture the plant is adorned with them.

Habitat/Range: The widespread honey mesquite often assumes dominance in low sandy areas. This species has increased greatly in our area due to disturbance, elimination of native plants, and spread of the seeds that pass through the digestive tracts of cattle. BBNP, CCNP, FDHS, GMNP, WSNM.

Comments: Honey mesquite is an important wildlife plant, with many species eating the seeds, others taking the nectar, and others using it for browse or shelter.

Screwbean mesquite.

SCREWBEAN MESQUITE
Prosopis pubescens
Legume Family (Fabaceae)

Description: Four to eight pairs of leaflets appear on each compound leaf. The pale yellow flowers bloom from May through June, occasionally into early September. The best way to identify this plant is by the presence of the spiral seedpod containing many small seeds.

Habitat/Range: Less widespread than the honey mesquite, screwbean mesquite is found in our area primarily in alluvial soil along the Rio Grande drainage and other localities. BBNP, GMNP.

Comments: Wildlife use this species much as they do honey mesquite, and it also provides important nesting habitat for white-winged doves along the Rio Grande. It is locally known as *tornillo* (screw).

Desert poppy.

BETTY ALEX

DESERT POPPY
Kallstroemia grandiflora
Caltrop Family (Zygophyllaceae)

Description: This locally common annual often grows in clumps almost 6 ½' (2 m) across, climbing over surrounding plants and rocks. Distinguishing characters are the generally prostrate, hairy branches and compound opposite leaves with elliptical leaflets in five to ten pairs. The bright yellow-orange flowers occasionally have a reddish center. These large, solitary flowers occur from March to as late as November.

Habitat/Range: Desert poppy is most often found at lower elevations on gravelly soils. BBNP, CCNP.

Comments: Dove feed on the seeds; it is also known as Mexican poppy.

GEORGE O. MILLER

Creosotebush.

CREOSOTEBUSH
Larrea tridentata
Caltrop Family (Zygophyllaceae)

Description: An aromatic shrub, creosotebush gives off a pleasant and distinct odor after a desert rain. The plant can grow up to 13' (4 m) tall but is generally 3' (1 m) high or less. The thick, waxy evergreen leaves shine in the sunlight, the coating helping to retard evaporation. The bright yellow flowers bloom primarily in April and May and later develop into white, fuzzy fruits.

Habitat/Range: Creosotebush is a dominant plant in our area, especially at lowland, overgrazed sites. BBNP, CCNP, GMNP, WSNM.

Comments: Bees are an important pollinator, and one species of grasshopper feeds exclusively on creosotebush. Used widely in the past for various disorders, the plant has undergone contemporary research for possible medical uses. The leaf coating is high in antioxidants, which may prove beneficial against some cancers. Creosotebush occupies more than 70,000 square miles (112,903 sq km) of southwestern desert. One specimen in the Mojave Desert has been dated at 9400 years, the oldest individual plant known on Earth.

STINGING CEVALLIA
Cevallia sinuata
Stickleaf Family (Loasaceae)

Description: The overwhelming abundance of stinging hairs covering the stems, leaves, and flowers deter browsers. Small yellowish flowers in spherical heads, blooming from May to October, generally open in early morning and close as the day warms.

Habitat/Range: This species is often locally common, especially in gypsum areas. Elsewhere, it is most frequently found in rocky places but is somewhat limited in numbers. BBNP, CCNP, FDHS, GMNP, WSNM.

GEORGE O. MILLER

Stinging cevallia.

LAURENCE PARENT

Yellow rocknettle.

YELLOW ROCKNETTLE
Eucnide bartonioides
Stickleaf Family (Loasaceae)

Description: The large, bright yellow flowers with numerous projecting stamens bloom from March to August, although some have been recorded blooming in November and January. Dark green, triangular leaves with irregular margins help identify it when it is not in flower.

Habitat/Range: This is one of the more striking flowers in our area and can be seen along the Rio Grande floodplain, primarily in Big Bend National Park. Check cliff faces at Hot Springs in the park. BBNP, GMNP.

Comments: Do not handle this plant—the stinging hairs are vicious. Also known as Warnock's rock nettle.

BRENT WAUER

Desert mentzelia.

DESERT MENTZELIA
Mentzelia multiflora
Stickleaf Family (Loasaceae)

Description: Unlike the other two genera from this family treated here, *Cevallia* and *Eucnide*, *Mentzelia* species do not have stinging hairs. Instead the leaves possess tiny pagoda-shaped hairs with barbs on the edges that will cling to almost anything with which they come in contact (you can see these hairs with a hand lens). *Mentzelia* are also characterized by a thin, paperlike epidermis on the plant's stalks that easily peels off. The bright yellow flowers occur from March to occasionally as late as October.

Habitat/Range: This species is frequently found on disturbed sites. BBNP, CCNP, GMNP, WSNM.

CHICKEN THIEF
Mentzelia oligosperma
Stickleaf Family (Loasaceae)

Description: This erect perennial grows up to 1' (0.3 m) tall. As the plant develops, the stems gradually become whitish. The orange, sometimes yellow-orange flowers are pollinated by bees during the day and by moths at night. This species blooms from May to September, sometimes in October.

Habitat/Range: It is found in a wide variety of soils but is most common in limestone. BBNP, CCNP, FDHS, GMNP.

Comments: Also known as *pegajosa* (sticky, as in sticky fingers).

BRENT WAUER

Chicken thief.

SAND STICKLEAF
Mentzelia strictissima
Stickleaf Family (Loasaceae)

Description: This is one of the tallest *Mentzelia*, growing as tall as 3' (1 m). The large, white flowers bloom from late May to sometimes as late as October. As with other species, the flowers open in late afternoon.

Habitat/Range: The plant generally occurs in sandy soil. CCNP.

Sand stickleaf.

Hartweg's evening primrose.

HARTWEG'S EVENING PRIMROSE
Calylophus hartwegii
Evening Primrose Family (Onagraceae)

Description: This low-growing plant produces a bright yellow flower from April to September and occasionally into October.

Habitat/Range: This evening primrose can be common and conspicuous in our area, particularly along disturbed roadsides and in gypsum areas. It is also locally abundant on limestone at lower elevations. BBNP, CCNP, GMNP, WSNM.

Comments: The flower opens in the afternoon through the evening, attracting hawk moths and hummingbirds.

BRENT WAUER

Stemless aletes.

STEMLESS ALETES
Aletes acaulis
Parsley Family (Apiaceae)

Description: The simple leaflets and single compound flower umbel on a leafless stem help identify this plant. The yellow flowers bloom from April to August, occasionally as late at October. The plant is up to 14" (35 cm) tall.

Habitat/Range: This perennial herb is infrequently found in rocky areas at higher elevations. BBNP.

HAIRY FALSE NIGHTSHADE
Chamaesaracha sordida
Nightshade Family (Solanaceae)

Description: This perennial herb is usually low growing but will branch upward to 8" (20 cm). The sticky, glandular stems and leaves attract grains of sand and dirt, giving the plant a dirty appearance. Lobed leaves are scattered along the stems. The greenish yellow flowers can be solitary or in small clusters. The corolla has five short, broad lobes. This plant blooms from May to October.

Habitat/Range: This is the most likely member of this genus to be encountered in our area. It occurs in a variety of habitats, most commonly on dry plains and gradual slopes, especially on limestone outcrops. BBNP, CCNP, GMNP.

Comments: Reportedly browsed by deer; it is also known as prostrate groundcherry.

NPS PHOTO

Hairy false nightshade.

BRENT WAUER

Tree tobacco.

TREE TOBACCO
Nicotiana glauca
Nightshade Family (Solanaceae)

Description: This plant appears either as a shrub or slender tree and is commonly up to 13' (4 m) tall. The long, yellow, tubular flower, blooming from April through November, makes the plant easy to identify. The smooth leaves are up to 6" (15 cm) long.

Habitat/Range: Tree tobacco is an introduced species native to South America. It is now widespread along the Rio Grande of Big Bend National Park and is occasionally encountered elsewhere in western Texas. Though it does not occur in southeastern New Mexico, it can be found along the Rio Grande at Las Cruces. It occurs most frequently along floodplains but also is found on roadsides and in disturbed areas. BBNP.

Comments: Tree tobacco produces an insecticide that practical gardeners can use to deter aphids. Hummingbirds frequently visit the flowers.

BRENT WAUER

Five-flowered rock-daisy.

FIVE-FLOWERED ROCK-DAISY
Perityle quinqueflora
Sunflower Family (Asteraceae)

Description: This is a perennial, growing up to 1' (30 cm) tall from a woody base. The triangular or kidney-shaped leaves are opposite below and sometimes alternate toward the top of the plant. The yellow flowers bloom from April to October.

Habitat/Range: This species is limited in range and restricted mostly to limestone. In our area it is most easily found in Walnut and Slaughter Canyons between 3937' (1200 m) to 6070' (1850 m) elevation in the Guadalupe Mountains. CCNP, GMNP.

TRUMPETFLOWER
Tecoma stans
Catalpa Family (Bignoniaceae)

Description: Trumpetflower is usually 3' (1 m) or less in height and is characterized by having many stems and hairless compound leaves with toothed margins. The large bright yellow flowers, in bloom from May to October, help identify the plant.

Habitat/Range: This small shrub is limited in our area mainly to Big Bend National Park and parts of the Davis Mountains. It is widespread in igneous and limestone soils and is especially frequent on rocky hillsides. BBNP, FDHS.

Comments: Native Americans reportedly made bows from the wood, and extracts have been mentioned as useful in treating syphilis, stomach cramps, and diabetes. Also known as *esperanza* (hope).

F. D. EVANS

Trumpetflower.

Coyote melon.

COYOTE MELON
Cucurbita foetidissima
Gourd Family (Cucurbitaceae)

Description: The specific name, *foetidissima,* describes the odor of the plant, which is readily noticeable when walking through a group of these vines. The large yellow flowers, the trailing vines with triangular leaves, and the green gourd (yellow when ripe) help to identify this plant.

Habitat/Range: This is often a fairly common or at least obvious perennial in our area, especially along roadsides. It grows in scattered locations in the parks and is easily found at Rattlesnake Springs in Carlsbad Caverns National Park. BBNP, CCNP, FDHS, GMNP, WSNM.

Comments: The large tuber stores water and nutrients that sustain the plant through dry periods. Also known as buffalo gourd and *calabacilla.*

Desert marigold.

DESERT MARIGOLD
Baileya multiradiata
Sunflower Family (Asteraceae)

Description: The bright yellow flowers are up to 2" (5 cm) across and are composed of 25 to 50 ray flowers. Broad oval leaves are grouped together at the base of stems, several of which may arise from the base of the plant. The stems and leaves have numerous white, woolly hairs. The stems are usually around 8" (20 cm) tall. It blooms almost throughout the year but most frequently from April through November

Habitat/Range: Desert marigold can be locally common. This species is found in sandy and rocky areas and is an important colonizer of disturbed areas. BBNP, CCNP, GMNP.

LYRELEAF GREENEYES
Berlandiera lyrata
Sunflower Family (Asteraceae)

Description: Except for basal leaves, this plant is largely leafless. Leaves have scalloped edges. Yellow ray flowers surround the maroon disk, with the whole flower head about 1 ½" (4 cm) across. Flowers occur from April to October and have a distinctive chocolate fragrance.

Habitat/Range: The species occurs widely as individuals or in groups in grassy limestone areas at low to middle elevations throughout the northern Chihuahuan Desert. BBNP, CCNP, FDHS, GMNP.

Comments: Native Americans reportedly used this species for seasoning foods. Also known as chocolate daisy.

Lyreleaf greeneyes.

CUTLEAF BRICKLEBUSH
Brickellia laciniata
Sunflower Family (Asteraceae)

Description: This shrub, up to 5' (1.5 m) tall, has green to light yellow flowers that appear from August to as late as November. Limbs of the shrub sometimes appear to be tinged with purple. Narrow leaves crowd the stems.

Habitat/Range: It is usually quite common and is most frequently encountered along arroyos in gravelly soil and other low spots where moisture may accumulate. It is often more abundant in disturbed areas. BBNP, CCNP, GMNP.

BRENT WAUER

Cutleaf bricklebush.

RICK LOBELLO

Damianita.

DAMIANITA
Chrysactinia mexicana
Sunflower Family (Asteraceae)

Description: Damianita has very short, narrow leaves. The golden yellow flower heads, usually with eight narrow ray flowers, occur on slender stalks from June to October. This strongly scented shrub, which grows up to 8" (20 cm) tall.

Habitat/Range: This is a locally occurring shrub found mostly on limestone but also in igneous areas. It can be found up to about 6562' (2000 m) elevation. BBNP, CCNP, FDHS.

BRENT WAUER

Common dogweed.

COMMON DOGWEED
Dyssodia pentachaeta
Sunflower Family (Asteraceae)

Description: This perennial is woody at the base with mostly paired, needlelike leaves. The plant is small but erect, reaching up to 10" (25 cm) in height. Each of the numerous branches are tipped with many yellow flowers with elevated yellow centers. The head of the flower is about ½" (1.3 cm) across, with eight to thirteen ray flowers.

Habitat/Range: It occurs on dry slopes from 2460' to 4593' (750 m to 1400 m) in elevation. BBNP, CCNP.

Comments: Also known as *parralnea*.

TARBUSH
Flourensia cernua
Sunflower Family (Asteraceae)

Description: Tarbush is abundant at lower elevations in the northern Chihuahuan Desert and is sometimes considered an indicator species of this desert. The shrub grows up to 6 ½' (2 m) high and produces simple, alternate, persistent leaves. The yellow flowers bloom from July through December, with a peak in October.

Habitat/Range: It ranges up to 4921' (1500 m), though in decreasing densities. BBNP, CCNP, FDHS, GMNP, WSNM.

Comments: Tarbush often grows in association with creosotebush.

BARTON WARNOCK

Tarbush.

GYP INDIAN-BLANKET
Gaillardia multiceps
Sunflower Family (Asteraceae)

Description: This perennial has a woody base and ranges up to 14" (35 cm) tall. Leaves occur at the base of the plant. The disk flowers are red while the ray flowers are yellow and three-lobed. The plant blooms from June through September.

Habitat/Range: As the common name implies, this species is found predominantly on gypsum soil at low elevations. GMNP.

Gyp Indian-blanket.

REDDOME BLANKETFLOWER
Gaillardia pinnatifida
Sunflower Family (Asteraceae)

Description: Bright yellow ray flowers surround a purple to dark red center of disk flowers. Flowers are present from May to October. This perennial herb grows up to 16" (40 cm) in height.

Habitat/Range: This attractive *Gaillardia* can be locally abundant in grasslands up to 6890' (2100 m) elevation. It is found most frequently on limestone but also occurs on other soils. BBNP, CCNP, FDHS, GMNP.

Comments: Also known as old red eye.

Reddome blanketflower.

Curly-cup gumweed.

CURLY-CUP GUMWEED
Grindelia squarrosa
Sunflower Family (Asteraceae)

Description: Curly-cup gumweed is an openly branched annual that can be common, especially in overgrazed pastures. The plant is topped with numerous flower heads. Sticky flower bracts hold tightly to the flower and are rolled back. The flower is usually less than 1 ½" (4 cm) across with a small area occupied by the disk flowers. Both the disk and ray flowers are yellow. The flowering period ranges from June to October. Leaves with sharply serrated edges clasp the stem.

Habitat/Range: CCNP, GMNP.

Comments: Curly-cup gumweed can absorb selenium from the soil and becomes poisonous to animals that feed on it. The plant was widely used by Native Americans and pioneers to treat various illnesses, including asthma, kidney disorders, and sores.

THREADLEAF BROOMWEED
Gutierrezia microcephala
Sunflower Family (Asteraceae)

Description: Threadleaf broomweed and broom snakeweed are very similar, and both have increased greatly in the past century due to overgrazing and other land use practices. Threadleaf broomweed is generally shorter and has loose clusters of flower heads with two to three, occasionally four, ray flowers. Flowers bloom from June through October. The plant grows to 3' (1 m) tall and at least 3' (1 m) wide, so it looks rounded. The numerous slender branches at the base are covered with many slender, alternate leaves.

Habitat/Range: It grows at elevations of 2543' (775 m) to 6004' (1830 m). BBNP, CCNP, GMNP, WSNM.

Comments: This plant is toxic to cattle and other livestock.

Threadleaf broomweed.

BROOM SNAKEWEED
Gutierrezia sarothrae
Sunflower Family (Asteraceae)

Description: This species is a perennial herb similar to threadleaf broomweed, which also has alternate leaves, a woody base, and mostly erect stems. Broom snakeweed, however, has three to seven ray flowers and two to six disk flowers. The flower heads occur in tight clusters and appear from June to October. The plant can be 3' (1 m) tall.

Habitat/Range: It has greatly increased across the northern Chihuahuan Desert over the past hundred years. BBNP, CCNP, FDHS, GMNP, WSNM.

Comments: Native Americans were reported to use this plant medicinally to treat snakebite, ant bites, and bee and wasp stings.

Broom snakeweed.

Common sunflower.

COMMON SUNFLOWER
Helianthus annuus
Sunflower Family (Asteraceae)

Description: The flowers bloom from March through October and have golden yellow petals with large purple-brown centers. The plant is tall, up to 9' (3 m). Alternate, rough, toothed leaves grow on a hairy stem.

Habitat/Range: Common sunflower is the most widespread and frequently noted sunflower in our area. It is found throughout a wide range of elevations, generally in dry open areas including plains, roadsides, and foothills. BBNP, CCNP, WSNM.

Comments: The seeds feed many birds, and Native Americans made a yellow dye from the flowers. Also known as *mirasol* (sun-watcher).

LEWIS EPPLE

Plains sunflower.

PLAINS SUNFLOWER
Helianthus petiolaris
Sunflower Family (Asteraceae)

Description: Plants are less than 6 ½' (2 m) tall. The flower heads are smaller than the common sunflower, and the disk flowers have a white spot in the center. Plains sunflower blooms from June through October. The leaf blades are generally only half as broad as long, and the plant is not as hairy as is the common sunflower.

Habitat/Range: The plains and common sunflower are similar, but the plains sunflower is more likely to be found in sand dune areas. BBNP, CCNP, GMNP, WSNM.

MOUNTAIN OXEYE
Heliopsis parvifolia
Sunflower Family (Asteraceae)

Description: This flower is an erect perennial herb up to 16" (40 cm) in height. The coarse leaves are lance-shaped to oval. Orange-gold ray and disk flowers are present and are about 2" (5 cm) across. This species blooms from July to November.

Habitat/Range: Unfortunately for wildflower enthusiasts, this handsome flower is only found locally in the mountains of the northern Chihuahuan Desert. BBNP.

JEAN HARDY

Mountain oxeye.

RAYLESS GOLDENROD
Isocoma wrightii
Sunflower Family (Asteraceae)

Description: Rayless goldenrod is a perennial, producing alternate linear leaves and numerous stems from a somewhat woody base. The ascending plant is usually about 27" (69 cm) tall or less. Many yellow flower heads form a thick inflorescence at the tip of the stems. Flowers can be found from June through late September. This plant often occurs in overgrazed areas, along roadsides and abandoned fields.

Habitat/Range: This locally abundant species seems to grow best in alkaline localities and dry areas. Rayless goldenrod is highly toxic to sheep, cattle, and horses. This large composite makes an attractive ornamental. BBNP, GMNP, WSNM.

Rayless goldenrod.

CUTLEAF GOLDENWEED
Machaeranthera pinnatifida
Sunflower Family (Asteraceae)

Description: The lower two-thirds of the stem is rigid, while the ends are more flexible. The leaves are pinnately cleft. Many branches start toward the tip of the stem, each of which terminates in a bright yellow flower. Flowers occur from May through September.

Habitat/Range: This common perennial herb is found throughout our area, especially where limestone occurs. BBNP, CCNP, FDHS.

Cutleaf goldenweed.

RICK LOBELLO

Lemonweed.

LEMONWEED
Pectis angustifolia
Sunflower Family (Asteraceae)

Description: Lemonweed is usually less than 8" (20 cm) tall. Lemonweed is covered with thick, grasslike leaves, and the leaves and flower bracts are covered with glands that provide the lemony aroma characteristic of this plant. The yellow flower heads, bunched at the ends of the branches, occur from June through October. Flowers are about 1 ⅜" (3.5 cm) across and have eight to ten short rays.

Habitat/Range: This annual is often widespread in our area at low to middle elevations ranging up to 6890' (2100 m). BBNP, CCNP, WSNM.

Comments: Also known as *limoncillo*.

WOOLLY PAPER-FLOWER
Psilostrophe tagetina
Sunflower Family (Asteraceae)

Description: This perennial is usually shorter than 19" (48 cm). The lower leaves are larger and less green than the ones toward the top of the plant. The bright yellow flowers generally cover the top of the plant and occur from April through October. The ray flowers are three-lobed; as they mature they develop a papery, woolly appearance, thus the name.

Habitat/Range: This flower grows in open areas up to at least 6890' (2100 m) elevation. BBNP, CCNP, GMNP, WSNM.

LEWIS EPPLE

Woolly paper-flower.

Mexican hat.

BRENT WAUER

MEXICAN HAT
Ratibida columnaris
Sunflower Family (Asteraceae)

Description: This highly variable species requires more moisture than some other Chihuahuan Desert species, and adequate rain can produce thick blooms of this coneflower from May through November. The dark red to dark purple disk flowers occur on an upright column. The ray flowers vary from bright yellow to reddish brown and shades in between. Plants growing in the more southerly part of the range tend to have darker ray flowers. Leaf blades are divided into as many as nine segments. The seed heads are very aromatic when crushed.

Habitat/Range: Mexican hat is locally abundant at a wide range of elevations in our area. BBNP, CCNP, FDHS, GMNP.

Comments: Also known as prairie coneflower.

Threadleaf groundsel.

THREADLEAF GROUNDSEL
Senecio douglasii
Sunflower Family (Asteraceae)

Description: The alternate leaves are divided into three to seven segments. The stems are whitish. Individuals can grow up to 3' (1 m) in height. Bright yellow flower heads, relatively few in number, bloom during any month of the year but are most frequent spring through fall.

Habitat/Range: Threadleaf groundsel is sometimes split into two separate species, *Senecio douglasii* and *S. longilobus*. This many-branched, perennial herb is common in the northern Chihuahuan Desert up to about 7000' (2130 m) elevation. BBNP, CCNP, FDHS, GMNP, WSNM.

Comments: This species is poisonous to livestock and increases rapidly in abused land or disturbed areas.

TALL GOLDENROD
Solidago altissima
Sunflower Family (Asteraceae)

Description: Tall goldenrod grows from a horizontal rootstock and can be as high as 6 ½' (2 m). Stems are numerous, and the crowded leaves are simple and alternate. Many yellow flower heads are generally crowded onto one side of each of the arching branches at the top of the plant. Flowers occur from July through November.

Habitat/Range: It is most often found in wet places at 5000' (1524 m) elevation and higher. CCNP.

Comments: This perennial and the other tall goldenrod, *Solidago sparsiflora*, are often maligned as "hay-fever plants," but the culprit is actually an inconspicuous *Ambrosia*, a bursage, which is a low, shrubby member of the aster family that blooms at the same time.

Tall goldenrod.

ROUGH GOLDENROD
Solidago sparsiflora
Sunflower Family (Asteraceae)

Description: Rough goldenrod is usually 3'
(1 m) or less tall. The leaves are sparingly
toothed, with the middle and upper leaves
being smaller than the lower ones. The yellow
blooms, which appear from June through October, are numerous on the curving spikes.

Habitat/Range: This perennial occurs locally
throughout the northern Chihuahuan Desert
at elevations generally above 4003' (1220 m).
BBNP.

Rough goldenrod.

COMMON DANDELION
Taraxacum officinale
Sunflower Family (Asteraceae)

Description: Dandelion is identified by the
presence of basal leaves with a single, hollow
stem, topped by a terminal yellow flower. The
flower can be 6" (15 cm) above the ground.
The flower matures into a globe of mature
"parachute" fruits that are scattered by the
wind.

Habitat/Range: The common dandelion is
one plant everyone with a lawn knows quite
well. This introduced perennial does well even
in the relatively dry northern Chihuahuan
Desert. It grows at all elevations and flourishes
in disturbed areas. CCNP, GMNP.

Common dandelion.

BRENT WAUER

Goat's beard.

GOAT'S BEARD

Tragopogon dubius
Sunflower Family (Asteraceae)

Description: Overall, this plant resembles a giant dandelion. There is a large head of bright yellow ray flowers that generally open only during the morning. They bloom from May through July. As the plant matures, it develops a large ball of brown seedlike fruits attached to extended parachutes that are carried by the wind or an animal's fur. The broken stems produce a milky latex.

Habitat/Range: This introduced species is frequently common along roadsides, in abandoned fields, and in disturbed areas. In our area it is generally widespread in such habitats at all elevations. CCNP, GMNP.

BUFFALO BUR

Solanum rostratum
Nightshade Family (Solanaceae)

Description: The dense yellow prickles on the plant, the large yellow flower, and the lobed leaves readily identify this species, as does the spiny yellow bur that encloses the seeds. Buffalo bur blooms from late April to early October. The immature plant is often mistaken for a young tomato or watermelon.

Habitat/Range: Like silverleaf nightshade, buffalo bur is often found in disturbed areas, though generally it is not as dense as silverleaf nightshade. It can be an aggressive invader in abandoned fields and overgrazed areas, where it becomes widespread for a year or two but gradually declines. BBNP, CCNP, GMNP.

Comments: This plant is reported to be toxic and is rarely grazed.

LEWIS EPPLE

Buffalo bur.

LONG-STALK GREENTHREAD
Thelesperma longipes
Sunflower Family (Asteraceae)

Description: This strongly scented perennial grows up to about 2' (60 cm) in height. Leaves are slender and grow mostly at the base of the plant. The long stalk is topped with a small yellow flower about ⅜" (1 cm) across that lacks ray flowers. The flowers are in bloom from May to November.

Habitat/Range: Long-stalk greenthread occurs widely throughout the northern Chihuahuan Desert at low to middle elevations, most frequently in limestone soils. BBNP, CCNP, GMNP.

Long-stalk greenthread.

Slender greenthread.

SLENDER GREENTHREAD
Thelesperma megapotamicum
Sunflower Family (Asteraceae)

Description: Slender greenthread is larger than long-stalk greenthread, often being 3' (1 m) tall. It is a perennial herb that produces basal leaves and few branches. The disk flowers are yellow, although some are maroon; there are no ray flowers. Blooming occurs from May to October.

Habitat/Range: This species grows at elevations up to 6890' (2100 m) and is more likely to be found on igneous or gypsum soils. BBNP, CCNP, FDHS, GMNP, WSNM.

BRENT WAUER

Golden crownbeard.

GOLDEN CROWNBEARD
Verbesina encelioides
Sunflower Family (Asteraceae)

Description: This plant is best identified by the silver-gray foliage and the triangular, mostly paired leaves with toothed margins. The stems develop many branches, which give the plant a dense appearance. The plant can grow as tall as 3' (1 m). From April to November it produces attractive blossoms, with orange disk and yellowish orange ray flowers.

Habitat/Range: A widespread species common in disturbed areas, golden crownbeard grows more readily at lower elevations, but it can be found up to 7218' (2200 m). BBNP, CCNP, FDHS, GMNP, WSNM.

Comments: Native Americans and settlers often used this plant to treat skin ailments such as boils.

SUNFLOWER GOLDENEYE
Viguiera dentata
Sunflower Family (Asteraceae)

Description: This species blooms from June through November, with broad flowers that are about 1" (2.5 cm) across. It has mostly paired, oval leaves and grows up to 3' (1 m) tall.

Habitat/Range: This perennial herb occurs throughout the northern Chihuahuan Desert at elevations from 3281' (1000 m) to 6890' (2100 m). It can be very common locally and is most abundant on dry limestone hills, as in the Guadalupe Mountains. BBNP, CCNP, FDHS, GMNP.

GEORGE O. MILLER

Sunflower goldeneye.

LEWIS EPPLE

Longleaf goldeneye.

LONGLEAF GOLDENEYE
Viguiera longifolia
Sunflower Family (Asteraceae)

Description: The leaves are narrow and lance-shaped, broader than the other members of the genus covered here. The bright yellow disk and ray flowers occur from July to November.

Habitat/Range: This annual of dry areas at elevations of 3937' to 7546' (1200 m to 2300 m) is generally uncommon. BBNP, CCNP.

Skeleton-leaf goldeneye.

SKELETON-LEAF GOLDENEYE
Viguiera stenoloba
Sunflower Family (Asteraceae)

Description: Although some specimens can reach 6 ½' (2 m), most are about 4'4" (1.3 m) in height. The slender stalks bear solitary flower heads from June through October. The yellow ray flowers are deeply veined; the disk flowers range from yellowish brown to a golden color.

Habitat/Range: Skeleton goldeneye is a shrub found in limestone areas from 1969' to 6234' (600 m to 1900 m) elevation throughout our area. BBNP, CCNP, GMNP.

Comments: This plant, and probably other members of the genus, is at least irregularly browsed by deer and livestock during times of stress.

SPINYLEAF ZINNIA
Zinnia acerosa
Sunflower Family (Asteraceae)

Description: The white to creamy white ray flowers and yellow disk flowers help to identify this low plant, which reaches only about 6" (15 cm) high. It blooms from June through October and can be locally abundant.

Habitat/Range: Spinyleaf zinnia grows in grasslands, slopes, and flats, mostly in limestone, up to elevations of 5249' (1600 m). BBNP, CCNP, GMNP, WSNM.

Comments: Also known as dwarf zinnia.

Spinyleaf zinnia.

TREES, SHRUBS, AND OTHER PLANTS

This section includes trees and shrubs that normally do not display the typical flowers seen in other sections of this book. If you are unable to find a plant in this section and have a flower to look at, check one of the color sections. This section also includes a number of non-flowering plants.

BRENT WAUER

Resurrection plant.

RESURRECTION PLANT
Selaginella pilifera
Spikemoss Family (Selaginellaceae)

Description: Several species in this genus occur in the area. As a group these plants often appear dead and lifeless much of the time. Sufficient moisture, though, brings them "back to life," making the leaves uncurl and turn green, hence the common name.

Habitat/Range: They grow most commonly in rocky areas, especially where limestone predominates, but are often overlooked. BBNP, CCNP, GMNP.

Comments: Though often sold in gift shops, avoid purchasing them because their collection damages the desert. Also called resurrection fern.

HORSETAIL
Equisetum laevigatum
Horsetail Family (Equisetaceae)

Description: Silica grains in the stems give the plant a rough texture.

Habitat/Range: This ancestral species occurs in small patches in the northern Chihuahuan Desert wherever the water supply is steady, or even where soils stay moist much of the year. It is easy to find along Rattlesnake Creek, lower stretches of south McKittrick Canyon, and other moist areas. BBNP, CCNP, GMNP.

Comments: These plants are commonly overlooked, hidden among shrubs and grass. Also known as *cola de caballo* (horse tail). European settlers used it to scrub and clean things, thus another common name, scouring rush.

GEORGE O. MILLER

Horsetail.

RIICK LOBELLO

Maidenhair fern.

MAIDENHAIR FERN
Adiantum capillus-veneris
Fern Family (Polypodiaceae)

Habitat/Range: This widespread fern occurs throughout much of temperate North America, to northern South America and Eurasia, but it is local in the northern Chihuahuan Desert. In this area it is restricted to moist areas, particularly those with year-round water. Colonies are often found on limestone rocks, under or near waterfalls. BBNP, CCNP, GMNP.

Description: The soft-green leaves which are lanceolate to ovate are numerous in this delicate-looking fern. Petiole and rachis are thin and black resembling a fine wire.

RICK LOBELLO

Bulb cloakfern.

BULB CLOAKFERN
Notholaena sinuata
Fern Family (Polypodiaceae)

Description: The fronds remain curled for most of the year until rains cause them to open and make the plant noticeable.

Habitat/Range: Although common, bulb cloakfern is often overlooked. Bulb cloakfern is most readily found sheltered by boulders, usually igneous or limestone rocks. BBNP, CCNP, GMNP.

STANDLEY CLOAKFERN
Notholaena standleyi
Fern Family (Polypodiaceae)

Description: This species is similar to the bulb cloakfern. However, on Standley cloakfern, the blades are triangular to pentagonal.

Habitat/Range: Standley cloakfern, also known as star cloakfern, is most frequently found in limestone areas. BBNP.

Comments: As with bulb cloakfern, it is often overlooked except following summer and early fall rains.

Standley cloakfern.

PONDEROSA PINE
Pinus ponderosa
Pine Family (Pinaceae)

Description: Ponderosa pine is identified by the yellowish bark, upright stance, and leaves (needles) in groups of three (sometimes in pairs).

Habitat/Range: The majestic ponderosa pine is conspicuous in mountainous areas, from ridgetops to sheltered limestone canyons with good drainage. It is rare at lower elevations. Ponderosas are more common in Guadalupe Mountains National Park than other parks in the area. In this part of its range the species can be more than 100' (30 m) in height, while individuals in other places can exceed 160' (50 m). CCNP, GMNP.

Comments: This is probably the most common pine in the American West and is an important source of timber. Note that the pine that grows in the Chisos Mountains in Big Bend is Arizona pine, *Pinus arizonica*. It has long needles usually in groups of five, four, or occasionally three.

Ponderosa pine.

Mexican pinyon.

MEXICAN PINYON
Pinus cembroides
Pine Family (Pinaceae)

Description: The species is best identified by its having three (rarely four) needles per cluster. As a group, pinyons are best identified by the rounded, squat cones.

Habitat/Range: Also known as the three-needle pinyon, this hardy tree is restricted largely to the Chisos and Davis Mountains. This pinyon prefers dry igneous slopes. BBNP.

TWO-NEEDLE PINYON
Pinus edulis
Pine Family (Pinaceae)

Description: Needles occur in groups of two.

Habitat/Range: This slow-growing pinyon occurs in the northern part of the area, on dry slopes, and is common in parts of the Guadalupe Mountains. BBNP, CCNP, GMNP.

Comments: People gather the nuts, and animals, including pinyon jays, rely on the seeds for food. It is the official New Mexico state tree; in some parts of that state, it is in decline because of increasing urbanization and popularity of the wood for cooking and heating. Also known as New Mexico pinyon.

Two-needle pinyon.

Southwestern white pine.

SOUTHWESTERN WHITE PINE
Pinus strobiformis
Pine Family (Pinaceae)

Description: Ponderosa pine is similar, but the southwestern white pine has five needles per bundle, and the bark is whitish gray and smooth. It is a close relative of (and sometimes considered the same species as) limber pine, *P. flexilis*, which is a more widespread and northerly species.

Habitat/Range: This pine is restricted in our area to the Guadalupe and Davis Mountains. CCNP, GMNP.

Douglas-fir.

DOUGLAS-FIR
Pseudotsuga menziesii
Pine Family (Pinaceae)

Description: The cones of Douglas-fir hang down and bear fringed "ears" on the scales.

Habitat/Range: This tall conifer grows mostly on north-facing slopes at high elevations, where it has more available moisture due to lower evaporation. BBNP, CCNP, GMNP.

Comments: Douglas-fir is one of the most important timber trees in the United States. In our area, it is at the southern extension of its range and is uncommon. Douglas-fir can survive under adverse conditions such as fire and drought and often invades forest openings. It is not a true fir, whose cones stand upright on the stem and decompose as they mature.

Arizona cypress.

ARIZONA CYPRESS
Cupressus arizonica
Cypress Family (Cupressaceae)

Description: The round cones are diagnostic for this species.

Habitat/Range: The majestic Arizona cypress is widespread in Mexico and also has limited distribution from California to western Texas. In our area it is limited to the Chisos Moun-tains, where the state champion tree stands 112' (34 m) tall. The best place to see Arizona cypress in Big Bend National Park is in Boot Canyon. BBNP.

Comments: This tree is now widely planted as an ornamental and a windbreak.

NPS PHOTO

Alligator juniper.

ALLIGATOR JUNIPER
Juniperus deppeana
Cypress Family (Cupressaceae)

Description: Alligator juniper, or tascate, is the only juniper in this area that has a large, checkered bark pattern on trunks of mature trees, which makes the species easy to identify. The bluish, sometimes reddish, berries are an important food for a variety of birds and mammals.

Habitat/Range: These trees are fairly common at higher elevations in the mountains. Leaves are occasionally browsed by livestock. BBNP, CCNP, FDHS, GMNP.

DROOPING JUNIPER
Juniperus flaccida
Cypress Family (Cupressaceae)

Description: The drooping, wilted appearance makes the plant easy to identify. The dark reddish brown fruits contain four to twelve seeds.

Habitat/Range: In our area, drooping juniper only occurs in the Chisos Mountains, where it is common. BBNP.

Comments: "Drooping" forms of the Rocky Mountain juniper, *Juniperus scopulorum*, occur in the Guadalupes. In addition, a very rare, drooping form of alligator juniper has been found in the Davis and possibly the Guadalupe Mountains. Also known as weeping juniper.

RICK LOBELLO

Drooping juniper.

BRENT WAUER

One-seed juniper.

ONE-SEED JUNIPER
Juniperus monosperma
Cypress Family (Cupressaceae)

Description: The mature fruits, usually containing a single seed, are dark bluish purple.

Habitat/Range: This species is common through much of the area covered in this book. It was apparently more common in the past, and many of the trees at lower elevations are relatively young. BBNP, CCNP, FDHS, GMNP.

Comments: The fruits are an important winter food for sage thrashers and many other animals. Large concentrations of wintering sage thrashers in the Guadalupes usually coincide with a good berry crop. The fruit can be dried and ground to make a type of flour. Also known as *tascate*.

BRENT WAUER

Pinchot juniper.

PINCHOT JUNIPER
Juniperus pinchotti
Cypress Family (Cupressaceae)

Description: Pinchot juniper is identified by reddish berries and furrowed bark.

Habitat/Range: This species is very common in limestone soils in southeastern New Mexico and much of western Texas. Pinchot juniper, also known as redberry juniper, often does well in rocky areas including eroded sites. BBNP, CCNP, GMNP.

Comments: The tree sprouts from the stump when cut or burned, and it often increases in overgrazed areas. It is an important food source to animals. The wood has been widely used for fence posts, and the species is good for reforestation because of its regenerative qualities.

MORMON TEA
Ephedra trifurca
Joint-Fir Family (Ephedraceae)

Description: Generally a short, spiny shrub composed of thin green stems. Leaves are much reduced and grow only at the nodes.

Habitat/Range: This genus is common and widespread in the northern Chihuahuan Desert, with several species occurring here. It prefers rocky soils. BBNP, FDHS, GMNP, WSNM.

Comments: Mormon tea can form a large shrub if not overgrazed, but grazed individuals are barely noticeable. It will spring back to life once grazing pressure is reduced. The common name comes from the practice of brewing a weak tea from the plant for its reputed medicinal value. It is also known as longleaf ephedra.

BRENT WAUER

Mormon tea.

NARROWLEAF CATTAIL
Typha angustifolia
Cattail Family (Typhaceae)

Description: The elongate, flat leaves identify the genus while the size of the bare area separating male flowers (the powdery ones above) and female flowers (the brown ones below) identifies the species.

Habitat/Range: This widespread species is local in our area because of its preference for steady, slow-moving water. Narrowleaf cattail is found across much of Eurasia and North America. BBNP, CCNP, GMNP, WSNM.

Comments: Several animals feed on the rootstocks, and many birds use the rapid-growing springtime shoots for nesting cover. Native Americans and settlers used the fluffy down of the mature seeds for bedding; the new shoots are edible and taste similar to cucumber.

Narrowleaf cattail.

Goodding willow.

GOODDING WILLOW
Salix gooddingii
Willow Family (Salicaceae)

Description: The leaves and small branches are tinged with yellow.

Habitat/Range: Goodding willow is probably the most common native willow in the northern Chihuahuan Desert. Dependant on a reliable source of water, it is found only along watercourses. BBNP, CCNP, GMNP, WSNM.

Comments: The species was probably once more widespread but has been heavily impacted by dams, water drawdowns, and cattle grazing. Historically it provided a great deal of nesting habitat for many species of birds. This is sometimes considered the same species as black willow, *Salix nigra*, which is widespread on the eastern and western coasts.

WALT ANDERSON

Quaking aspen.

QUAKING ASPEN
Populus tremuloides
Willow Family (Salicaceae)

Description: Aspens are easily identified by their slender, white-barked trunks. They can be up to 32' (9.7 m) tall.

Habitat/Range: Quaking aspen is a relict species from cooler, wetter times. It is found very locally in our area, persisting in small patches only in the highest parts of the Guadalupe, Davis, and Chisos Mountains. BBNP, GMNP.

Comments: The species is widespread across the Northern Hemisphere. The common name comes from the trembling of the leaves when the wind blows them. Able to spread through clones that grow from the roots of parent trees, aspens often invade after a fire or clearcut.

WALT ANDERSON

Fremont cottonwood.

FREMONT COTTONWOOD
Populus fremontii
Willow Family (Salicaceae)

Description: This tree can be 100' (30 m) tall. Although similar to the Rio Grande cottonwood, Fremont cottonwood lacks the leaf glands and gummy buds of that species. Some hybridization between the two is suspected, serving to cloud the picture. In the Fremont cottonwood, male and female flowers occur on separate plants, with the female flowers producing seeds covered with white "cotton" aiding in dispersal by wind and water.

Habitat/Range: BBNP.

Comments: This and other cottonwoods and willows have been severely impacted by removal for fence posts and firewood and because the floods they need for germination have been stopped by dams. Seedlings must also compete with saltcedar and avoid being eaten or trampled by cattle. Most cottonwood communities that have survived are only a remnant of what was once present in the northern Chihuahuan Desert.

RICK LOBELLO

Rio Grande cottonwood.

RIO GRANDE COTTONWOOD
Populus deltoides
Willow Family (Salicaceae)

Description: The leaves are simple and alternate, with a broadly triangular (deltoid) to ovate shape. Noting the two or more prominent glands on the upper leaf blade where it joins the leaf's stem is an easy way to tell it from Fremont cottonwood. Flowers appear from February to May, with male and female flowers occurring on separate plants. This widespread cottonwood is large, with individual plants up to 100' (30 m) in height.

Habitat/Range: BBNP, CCNP, GMNP.

Comments: A variety of animals and birds feed on the young trees and the seeds. This species is important in erosion control and indicates a dependable water source.

ARIZONA WALNUT
Juglans major
Walnut Family (Juglandaceae)

Description: The leaflets occur in groups of 15 or less, while on the Mexican walnut they are in groups of more than 15. The fruits of Arizona walnut are also larger, and the leaves have coarse-toothed edges.

Habitat/Range: Arizona walnut is scattered throughout our area and is generally not as common as the Mexican walnut. It occurs in rocky canyon bottoms from 2133' (650 m) to 7480' (2280 m) in elevation. BBNP, GMNP.

LAURENCE PARENT

Arizona walnut.

Mexican walnut.

MEXICAN WALNUT
Juglans microcarpa
Walnut Family (Juglandaceae)

Description: This tree is usually shrubby, often growing from several trunks. In this area, it rarely reaches more than 32' (9.7 m) in height. The tree flowers in March and April before it produces leaves.

Habitat/Range: Dense stands of this species are often found in canyon bottoms mixed with other tree species. It is easily seen in Walnut Canyon, the canyon one drives through to reach the entrance to Carlsbad Cavern. BBNP, CCNP, FDHS, GMNP.

Comments: Also known as *nogal,* it is strongly aromatic. The nuts are hard and small with only a small amount of meat inside, but it is a useful wildlife food, especially for rock squirrels. The tree also provides nesting sites for birds, in particular the threatened Bell's vireo.

BRENT WAUER

Knowlton hop-hornbeam.

KNOWLTON HOP-HORNBEAM
Ostrya knowltonii
Birch Family (Betulaceae)

Description: This species is easily identified by leaves that are 1 ½-3 ½" (4-9 cm) long with serrated edges. The flowers appear before the leaves in spring and the plant produces catkins.

Habitat/Range: Generally uncommon, Knowlton hop-hornbeam is restricted in our area to the Guadalupe Mountains. CCNP, GMNP.

Comments: A similar species, the Chisos hornbeam *(Ostrya chisosensis),* is known only from the higher Chisos Mountains of Big Bend National Park. Its leaves are typically elliptic rather than roundish as in Knowlton hop-hornbeam.

ARIZONA WHITE OAK
Quercus arizonica
Beech Family (Fagaceae)

Description: Arizona white oak reaches 39' (12 m) in height, with a rounded top and wide branches. The leaves are at least twice as long as they are broad; the undersides are covered with light brown hairs.

Habitat/Range: In our area this species is apparently restricted to western Texas. It can be found from elevations of 5085' (1550 m) up. GMNP.

Comments: Arizona white oak hybridizes frequently with other oaks, especially gray oak; this sometimes makes a complete identification of a particular specimen impossible.

WALT ANDERSON

Arizona white oak.

GAMBEL OAK
Quercus gambelii
Beech Family (Fagaceae)

Description: The deeply lobed leaves are the best distinguishing character of Gambel oak. The upper leaf surfaces are smooth and the lower surfaces are hairy. Trees can be up to 49' (15 m) in height, with a diameter of 27" (69 cm). Male and female catkins appear on the same tree. The cup encloses half of the acorn.

Habitat/Range: Trees are found from 4003' (1220 m) to 8202' (2500 m) in elevation. BBNP, CCNP, GMNP.

Comments: Deer and birds eat the acorns. They were the preferred acorns of Native Americans in this area, who went to great effort to prepare them.

Gambel oak.

Gray oak.

GRAY OAK
Quercus grisea
Beech Family (Fagaceae)

Description: The grayish cast of the foliage and the lack of lobes on the leaves help identify this common species of oak. The relatively large, evergreen leaves are usually smooth margined.

Habitat/Range: Gray oak occurs throughout our area from about 3200' (1000 m) to 7800' (2400 m) in elevation. BBNP, CCNP, FDHS, GMNP.

Comments: As with other oaks, deer browse the leaves, and porcupines and many other animals feed on the acorns.

Chinkapin oak.

CHINKAPIN OAK
Quercus muehlenbergii
Beech Family (Fagaceae)

Description: The chinkapin oak is certainly a prime candidate for the handsomest oak in our area, because of its size, distinctive leaf shape, and spreading crown. The acorns are solitary or in pairs. The large leaves are obovate with undulate margins.

Habitat/Range: Primarily an eastern species, it occurs locally in the northern Chihuahuan Desert. A nice relict population exists at Oak Spring at Carlsbad Caverns National Park, and the tree is also found in canyon bottoms at Guadalupe Mountains National Park. This species usually grows in well-drained, protected areas up to about 7800' (2400 m) in elevation. BBNP, CCNP, GMNP.

Comments: The largest specimen in our area is an individual 62' (19 m) tall in Big Bend National Park, although most are only 16' (5 m) or less.

SCRUB OAK
Quercus pungens
Beech Family (Fagaceae)

Description: Scrub oak usually occurs as a shrub but can grow to tree size, up to 23' (7 m). Leaves are usually oblong and toothed, often markedly undulate, or with three to five lobes on each side. The upper side of the leaves is dark green and the lower is hairy.

Habitat/Range: This species, also known as sandpaper oak, occurs in dry limestone areas and sometimes on igneous soils. Elevation range is from 3527' (1075 m) to 6562' (2000 m). BBNP, CCNP, FDHS, GMNP.

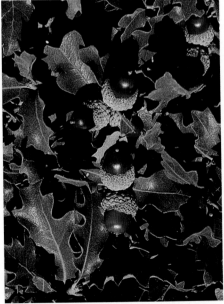

Scrub oak.

NETLEAF HACKBERRY
Celtis reticulata
Elm Family (Ulmaceae)

Description: Netleaf hackberry is identified most easily by the asymmetric, many-veined leaves, the smooth bark with numerous small knobs, and the reddish orange fruit.

Habitat/Range: This native elm is local in the Guadalupes and western Texas, mainly restricted to riparian areas and dry canyon bottoms at lower elevations, where thick stands can occur. BBNP, CCNP, FDHS, GMNP.

Comments: Native Americans once ate the fruit. Numerous species of birds and mammals, especially raccoons, also feed on the fruit. Hackberry trees also serve as important nesting sites and shelter for many birds.

GEORGE O. MILLER

Netleaf hackberry.

BRENT WAUER

Pine dwarf mistletoe.

PINE DWARF MISTLETOE
Arceuthobium vaginatum
Mistletoe Family (Viscaceae)

Description: The plants are leafless, range from orange to yellow, and have angled stems. A clump usually is less than 8" (20 cm) in diameter.

Habitat/Range: This parasitic plant is restricted to its host, the ponderosa pine. In our area it is found from 6234' (1900 m) to 7874' (2400 m) elevation. Out of our area it occurs from north-central Mexico north to Utah and Colorado. CCNP, GMNP.

Juniper mistletoe.

JUNIPER MISTLETOE
Phoradendron juniperinum
Mistletoe Family (Viscaceae)

Description: Dense groups of small flowers appear from July to September on stout, woody branches. The leaves are reduced to scales.

Habitat/Range: This shrubby mistletoe, a parasite, is restricted primarily to junipers and cypress. BBNP, CCNP, GMNP.

CHRISTMAS MISTLETOE
Phoradendron tomentosum
Mistletoe Family (Viscaceae)

Description: The branches are yellowish green and slightly hairy. Flowers occur from May through November.

Habitat/Range: This mistletoe is parasitic on a wide variety of plants, including hackberry, cottonwood, mesquite, acacia, oak, elm, willow, ash, and sycamore. BBNP, GMNP.

Comments: This is one of two species that parasitize local broad-leafed trees.

Christmas mistletoe.

OAK MISTLETOE
Phoradendron villosum
Mistletoe Family (Viscaceae)

Description: A dense covering of hairs gives the plant a light frosty appearance. Flowers occur from July through September.

Habitat/Range: This is one of our more common species of mistletoe, parasitizing oaks at elevations between 3445' (1050 m) and 6890' (2100 m). BBNP, CCNP, GMNP.

Oak mistletoe.

PICKLEWEED
Allenrolfea occidentalis
Goosefoot Family (Chenopodiaceae)

Description: This succulent shrub often grows up to 3' (1 m) tall.

Habitat/Range: This plant is limited in our area to highly saline soils. In wet years it can be the dominant plant along the edges of salt playas. Although found in a number of locations in western Texas and southern New Mexico, White Sands National Monument is the only National Park Service area in which it is at all common. It is marginal at Guadalupe Mountains National Park, the only other park where it is found. GMNP, WSNM.

Comments: This plant holds little forage value.

Pickleweed.

Common winter-fat.

COMMON WINTER-FAT
Eurotia lanata
Goosefoot Family (Chenopodiaceae)

Description: The plant grows up to 3' (1 m) tall. It has many stems with small leaves that are covered with whitish hairs.

Habitat/Range: This perennial shrub is generally not common, but the dense white foliage makes it conspicuous where it does occur. CCNP, GMNP.

Comments: A valuable forage plant, it is eaten by a wide variety of browsing animals throughout the winter.

PIGWEED
Amaranthus palmeri
Amaranth Family (Amaranthaceae)

Description: The alternate leaves and the spike of flowers identify this plant. The blooming period is long, depending on rainfall and temperature, and can last from June to November.

Habitat/Range: Pigweed, or Palmer amaranth, is a common annual in scattered locations throughout our area. It occurs in a wide variety of soils and can form dense stands in disturbed areas. BBNP, CCNP, FDHS, GMNP.

Comments: At times pigweed provides an important source of winter feed for birds. Native Americans gathered the green leaves and seeds for food.

Pigweed.

Guayacan.

GEORGE O. MILLER

GUAYACAN
Guaiacum angustifolium
Caltrop Family (Zygophyllaceae)

Description: Guayacan is rarely taller than 6 ½' (2 m). It can form thick growths. The leaves are pinnately compound with four to eight pairs of small, tough leaflets. The flower is a little more than ⅜" (1 cm) wide, with five purple to white petals with prominent yellow anthers. Two bright scarlet seeds are produced, and they are commonly eaten by wildlife and livestock.

Habitat/Range: This shrub is frequently encountered in Big Bend National Park around Rio Grande Village. The hard stems and dark green leaves often make it the most obvious large green bush at elevations below 4265' (1300 m). BBNP.

Comments: Wildlife browse on the plant. The bark has been reported as useful for washing wool fabric because it will not fade colors.

Desert sumac.

DESERT SUMAC
Rhus microphylla
Sumac Family (Anacardiaceae)

Description: This is a many-branched shrub or small tree usually less than 6 ½' (2 m) tall. The many small deciduous leaves are its most identifiable characteristic. Small whitish to green flowers appear before the leaves, from May to June. The twigs growing from the main branches are stiff and very spiny. The clusters of small bright red fruits are hairy.

Habitat/Range: Desert sumac is a wide-ranging plant, occurring from mountains to gypsum flats but most frequently in desert lowlands. BBNP, CCNP, FDHS, GMNP.

Comments: Sweet but somewhat acrid, the fruits are eaten by many birds and mammals. Mule deer also browse the plant. Also known as littleleaf sumac.

SKUNKBUSH
Rhus trilobata
Sumac Family (Anacardiaceae)

Description: From April to June, before the leaves appear, clusters of yellow to white flowers make the plant conspicuous. The three-lobed alternate leaves come in groups of three, and their odor when crushed is the characteristic that gives the plant its common name. The bright red to orange fruits are covered with short hairs.

Habitat/Range: This fairly common bush, up to 6 ½' (2 m) tall, is found at middle elevations in our area. Skunkbush sumac likes dry hillsides, canyons, and flats, decreasing in number as elevation increases. BBNP, CCNP, FDHS, WSNM.

Comments: The fruits are popular with birds, raccoons, and gray foxes.

Skunkbush.

NPS PHOTO

Bigtooth maple.

BIGTOOTH MAPLE
Acer grandidentatum
Maple Family (Aceraceae)

Description: The three- to five-lobed leaves have only a few widely spaced blunt teeth and are sometimes velvety beneath. Flowers occur during April and May. This species is rarely more than 19' (5.8 m) tall. It bears the characteristic fruit of the maple—two cells with wings—that can be dispersed by the wind. The bark is light brown to gray.

Habitat/Range: Bigtooth maple is the maple most likely to be encountered in our area, with populations widespread in Guadalupe Mountains National Park, the Chisos Mountains of Big Bend National Park, and similar highland areas. It grows in moist places, generally at the bottom of mountain canyons. BBNP, CCNP, GMNP.

Comments: Young plants are browsed by elk, deer, and livestock.

GEORGE O. MILLER

Javelina bush.

JAVELINA BUSH
Condalia ericoides
Buckthorn Family (Rhamnaceae)

Description: This shrub usually reaches 3' (1 m) or less in height. The plants are branched and very spiny. The leaves are alternate and very small. The fruit ranges in color from red to purplish when mature.

Habitat/Range: Javelina bush is a low-growing common shrub at lower elevations throughout our area. BBNP, CCNP, FDHS, GMNP.

Comments: Because of the thick texture, low height, and spines, this plant is generally not affected by grazing. The spininess and thickness might also limit its use as a food source, but many birds and mammals eat the fruits. Also known as *tecomblate*.

LOTEBUSH
Ziziphus obtusifolia
Buckthorn Family (Rhamnaceae)

Description: This shrub grows from 6 ½' to 13' (2 m to 4 m) tall and bears densely branched, gray twigs that are stiff and tipped with thorns. The creamy-white flowers occur from April to September. The leaves are oval. The single-seeded fruits turn deep purple as they ripen.

Habitat/Range: Lotebush can be locally common in dry, well-drained places such as arroyos and gravelly hillsides in much of our area, sometimes producing stands that are difficult to pass through. CCNP, GMNP.

Comments: It is eaten by a wide variety of birds and mammals, including gray fox and raccoon. Also known as graythorn.

BRENT WAUER

Lotebush.

CANYON GRAPE
Vitis arizonica
Grape Family (Vitaceae)

Description: The large maplelike leaves, many branches, coiled stems, and shredding bark help to identify canyon grape. The small white flowers occur in clusters. Tart dark purplish fruits mature in July to August but usually do not last long on the vine.

Habitat/Range: This many-tendriled vine occurs in limited locales in our area but can be locally common in gravelly or rocky soil, creeping over rocks, brush, and trees. BBNP, CCNP, FDHS, GMNP.

Comments: The fruits are consumed by a wide variety of birds and mammals.

BRENT WAUER

Canyon grape.

FREDERICK D. ATWOOD

Texas madrone.

TEXAS MADRONE
Arbutus xalapensis
Heath Family (Ericaceae)

Description: This plant is most easily identified by the pink to white bark, which peels off in paper-thin sheets. Each tree displays a unique bark pattern, and as the bark ages it becomes a rich brick red. The tree grows less than 33' (10 m) tall but is often more shrublike. The leathery leaves are alternate. White to pink, urnlike flowers appear from April to June and eventually produce reddish berries.

Habitat/Range: The widespread Texas madrone is one of the most beautiful plants of the northern Chihuahuan Desert, and in middle elevations is a conspicuous tree. BBNP, CCNP, FDHS, GMNP.

Comments: Birds eat the berries, and they are probably the most effective agents for distributing the seeds. This is an attractive ornamental that requires some shade from the afternoon sun. Also known as *manzanita* (small apple).

Velvet ash.

VELVET ASH
Fraxinus velutina
Olive Family (Oleaceae)

Description: The stalked leaflets occur in groups of five to nine. The leaves are darker green above. Yellow to green flowers appear on the tree in clusters before it starts producing leaves. The bark varies from gray to reddish. The tree can exceed 33' (10 m) in height.

Habitat/Range: Velvet ash occurs throughout our area in low numbers, especially where there is a steady supply of water, either surface or underground, such as in canyon bottoms. BBNP, CCNP, FDHS, GMNP.

Comments: Many birds and mammals eat the winged seeds.

COMMON HOREHOUND
Marrubium vulgare
Mint Family (Lamiaceae)

Description: The blooming period is long, April to September, producing many tiny flowers in tight circles around the square stems. Wrinkled, gray leaves grow along the white stem.

Habitat/Range: This introduced species can be very common throughout middle and lower elevations in our area. BBNP, CCNP, FDHS, GMNP.

Comments: Like most exotics, it does well in areas disturbed by people or cattle. Horehound is especially common around the entrance to Carlsbad Caverns and at Rattlesnake Springs.

Common horehound.

COMMON MULLEIN
Verbascum thapsus
Figwort Family (Scrophulariaceae)

Description: Oblong to lance-shaped leaves grow along a single erect stalk. It has a long blooming period stretching from March to as late as October.

Habitat/Range: Mullein is an introduced plant that occurs throughout the area, especially in canyon bottoms and on ridgetops. The seeds seem to germinate and establish best in disturbed areas, but the plant can be widespread. This plant is easily observed in McKittrick Canyon, along the Upper Loop Drive in Walnut Canyon, and on adjacent national forest land. CCNP, GMNP.

Comments: Also known as miner's candle.

Common mullein.

MEXICAN CANCER-ROOT
Conopholis mexicana
Broomrape Family (Orobanchaceae)

Description: The plant itself is up to 1' (30 cm) in height. It is mostly yellow with an erect, clublike stem. The lower stem is covered with yellow leaves that lack chlorophyll. The stem may be covered with many curved flowers from May to June, but frequently as early as March and as late as September.

Habitat/Range: This low-growing perennial herb, generally uncommon, is a parasite on oaks, pines, junipers, and possibly maples. BBNP, CCNP, FDHS, GMNP.

Comments: The common name arises from the use of members of this genus in folk medicine as a cancer remedy.

Mexican cancer-root.

BRENT WAUER

Woolly Indianwheat.

WOOLLY INDIANWHEAT
Plantago patagonica
Plantain Family (Plantaginaceae)

Description: The slender leaves and the flower stem are covered with long, dense, silky hairs. This plant grows up to 8" (20 cm) tall. This annual plantain blooms from early spring to late summer but occasionally as late as October.

Habitat/Range: BBNP, CCNP, GMNP.

Comments: Also known as Patagonia plantain.

COMMON COCKLEBUR
Xanthium strumarium
Sunflower Family (Asteraceae)

Description: Individual plants can be up to 6 ½' (2 m) tall. The leaves are 6" (15 cm) long and are almost as broad as they are long. The entire plant has a rough texture. Each plant bears separate male and female flowers; the female flowers, present from June through September, develop into the cocklebur, the seed case.

Habitat/Range: Common cocklebur is a widespread annual found in moist soils, although the distinctive seeds may turn up anywhere. BBNP, CCNP, GMNP.

Comments: The cocklebur seed is covered with long, curved spines that latch onto passing animals and aid in its dispersal. Also known as *abrojo* (thistle).

LEWIS EPPLE

Common cocklebur.

GLOSSARY

Alternate—occurring singly along a stem or axis.

Annual—a plant that completes its life cycle, from seed germination to production of new seeds, within a year and then dies.

Anther—that part of the stamen that has the pollen.

Awn—a slender, stiff bristle or fiber attached at its base to another part, such as a leaf tip.

Axil—the site where a leaf joins the stem.

Basal—at the base or bottom of; generally used in reference to leaves.

Biennial—a plant that completes its life cycle in two years; normally not producing flowers during the first year.

Bract—a reduced or modified leaf, often associated with flowers.

Bristle—a stiff hair, usually erect or curving away from its attachment point.

Bulb—an underground plant part derived from a short, usually rounded shoot that is covered with scales or leaves.

Calyx—the outer set of flower parts, composed of the sepals, which may be separate or joined together; usually green.

Capsule—a dry fruit that releases seeds through splits or holes.

Catkin—a dense, scaly spike of flowers.

Clasping—surrounding or partially wrapping around a stem or branch.

Cluster—any grouping or close arrangement of individual flowers that is not dense and continuous.

Compound Leaf—a leaf that is divided into two or more leaflets, each of which may look like a complete leaf but which lacks buds; may have leaflets arranged along an axis, like the rays of a feather, or radiating from a common point, like the fingers on a hand.

Conifer—a cone-bearing tree or shrub, usually evergreen.

Corolla—the set of flower parts interior to the calyx and surrounding the stamens and/or pistil and composed of the petals, which may be free or united; often brightly colored.

Disk Flower—a small, tubular flower in the central portion of the flower head of many plants in the sunflower family (Asteraceae).

Disturbed—referring to habitats that have been impacted by actions or processes associated with human settlement, such as ditching, grading, or long intervals of high-intensity grazing.

Divided—separated to the base.

Draw—a small, elongated depression with gentle side slopes in an upland landscape; resembles a miniature valley or ravine.

Ecosystem—a recognizable community of plants and animals affected by the same combination of environmental factors such as elevation, wind, temperature, precipitation, sunlight, soil type, and direction of slope.

Elliptic—oblong with rounded ends.

Erect—upright, standing vertically, or directly perpendicular from a surface.

Family—a group of plants having biologically similar features such as flower anatomy, fruit type, and so on. More closely related than members of an order (a higher category) and less so than the genus (a lower category).

Flower Head—as used in this guide, a dense and continuous group of flowers without obvious branches or space between them; used especially in reference to the sunflower family (Asteraceae).

Frond—a large compound leaf of a palm or a fern.

Generic Name—the first portion of a scientific name, identifying the genus in which the species belongs; for instance, in banana yucca, *Yucca baccata*, the generic name is *Yucca.*

Genus—a group of closely related species; for instance, the genus *Opuntia* encompasses all prickly pear cactus species.

Glochid—a minute barbed hair or bristle, as on prickly pear cactus.

Herbaceous—fleshy-stemmed; not woody.

Horn—a small rounded or flattened projection from the hoods of milkweed flowers.

Host—as used in this guide, a plant from which a parasitic plant derives nourishment.

Incurved—curved inwards, toward the stem.

Inversely Ovate—egg-shaped and attached at the narrow end.

Keel—the pair of lower, united petals on flowers typical of the legume family (Fabaceae).

Lance-shaped—elongate, narrowing to a point as in the head of a spear.

Linear—long and narrow, like a blade of grass.

Lobe—a segment of an incompletely divided plant part, typically rounded; often used in reference to leaves.

Margin—the edge of a leaf or petal.

Mat—plant growth that is low and densely interwoven or tangled.

Mesic—referring to a habitat that is well drained but generally moist throughout most of the growing season.

Node—a joint at a stem base, where leaves or stems arise.

Obovate—inversely ovate, growing wider towards the tip.

Opposite—paired directly across from one another along a stem or axis (*see* Alternate).

Ovary—the portion of the flower where the seeds develop; usually a swollen area below the style (if present) and stigma.

Ovate—egg-shaped.

Palmate—spreading like the fingers of a hand (*see* illustration p. 30).

Parallel—side by side, approximately the same distance apart, for the entire length; often used in reference to veins or edges of leaves.

Perennial—a plant that normally lives for three or more years.

Petal—the component parts of the corolla, often the most brightly colored and visible parts of the flower.

Pinnae—small leaflets, or major divisions of a pinnate leaf.

Pinnate—divided or lobed along each side of a leaf stalk, resembling a feather (*see* illustration p. 30).

Pistil—the seed-producing, or female, unit of a flower, consisting of the ovary, style (if present), and stigma; a flower may have one to several separate pistils.

Playa—the bed of a shallow, undrained lake that holds water only seasonally; when this water evaporates, mineral deposits are left behind.

Pod—a dry fruit that splits open along the edges.

Pollen—the tiny, often powdery, male repro

ductive cells formed in the stamens; typically necessary for seed production.

Prickle—a small, sharp, spinelike outgrowth.

Ray Flower—a flower in the sunflower family (Asteraceae) with a single, strap-shaped corolla resembling one flower petal; ray flowers may surround the disk flowers in a flower head, or in some species, such as dandelions, the flowers may be composed entirely of ray flowers (*see* illustration p. 34).

Recurved—curved away from, downward, or backward.

Rhizome—an underground stem producing roots and shoots at the nodes.

Runner—a long, trailing stem.

Sap—the juice within a plant.

Sedge—a large family of grasslike plants, many of which grow in wetlands.

Sepal—a component part of the calyx; typically green but sometimes enlarged and brightly colored.

Serrate—possessing sharp, forward-pointing teeth.

Shrub—a small, multistemmed, woody plant.

Simple Leaf—a leaf that has a single leaflike blade, although this may be lobed or divided (*see* illustration p. 30).

Specific Name—the second portion of a scientific name, identifying a particular species; for instance, in banana yucca, *Yucca baccata,* the specific name is *baccata.*

Spike—an elongated, unbranched cluster of stalkless or nearly stalkless flowers.

Spine—a thin, stiff, sharply pointed projection.

Spreading—extending outward from; at right angles to; widely radiating.

Spur—a hollow, tubular projection from the base of a petal or sepal; often produces nectar.

Stalk—as used here, the stem supporting the leaf, flower, or flower cluster.

Stalkless—lacking a stalk; describes leaves attached directly to the stem at the leaf base.

Stamen—the male unit of a flower, which produces the pollen; typically consisting of a long filament with a pollen-producing tip.

Standard—the usually erect, spreading, upper petal in flowers typical of the legume family (Fabaceae).

Sterile—in flowers, referring to an inability to produce seeds; in habitats, referring to poor nutrient and mineral availability in the soil.

Stigma—the portion of the pistil receptive to pollination; usually at the top of a style, and often appearing fuzzy or sticky.

Style—the stemlike portion of a pistil connecting the ovary and stigma.

Subspecies—a group of plants within a species that has consistent, genetically repeating qualitative or structural distinctions.

Succulent—thickened and fleshy or juicy.

Taproot—a stout, main root extending downward.

Terminal—occurring at the top or apex of a stem; usually refers to flowers or flower heads.

Toothed—bearing teeth or sharply angled projections along the edge.

Tuber—a thick, creeping underground stem; sometimes also used to describe thickened portions of roots.

Tubular—narrow, cylindrical, and tubelike.

Umbel—a convex to flat cluster of flowers.

Variety—a group of plants within a species that has a distinct range, habitat, or structure.

Veins—bundles of small tubes that carry water, minerals, and nutrients.

Whorl—three or more parts attached at the same point along a stem or axis and often surrounding the stem.

Winged—having thin bands of leaflike tissue attached edgewise along the length.

Woody—firm-stemmed or branched.

$\mathcal{S}$ELECTED REFERENCES

Bender, G. L., ed. 1982. *Reference Handbook on the Deserts of North America.* Westport, Conn.: Greenwood Press.

Correll, D. S., and M. C. Johnston. 1970. *Manual of the Vascular Plants of Texas.* Renner: Texas Research Foundation.

Dick-Peddie, W. A. 1993. *New Mexico Vegetation: Past, Present, and Future.* Albuquerque: University of New Mexico Press.

Echols, W. H. 1860. *Camel expedition through the Big Bend Country.* U.S. 26th Cong., 2d sess., Cong. Gov. vol. 2, report of October 10, 1860.

Gehlbach, F. R. 1967. "Vegetation of the Guadalupe Escarpment, New Mexico-Texas." *Ecology* 48:404-19.

Genoways, H. H., and R. J. Baker. 1979. *Biological Investigations in the Guadalupe Mountains National Park, Texas.* National Park Service Proceedings and Transactions Series no. 4. Washington, D.C.: U.S. Government Printing Office.

Henrickson, J., and R. M. Straw. 1976. *A Gazetteer of the Chihuahuan Desert Region: A Supplement to the Chihuahuan Desert Flora.* Los Angeles: California State University.

Herrera, E. A., and L. F. Huenneke, eds.1996. "New Mexico's Natural Heritage: Biological Diveristy in the Land of Enchantment." *New Mexico Journal of Science* 36:1-375.

Kearney, T. H., and R. H. Peebles. 1951. *Arizona Flora.* Berkeley and Los Angeles: University of California Press.

MacMahon, J. 1992. *Deserts.* National Audubon Society. New York: Alfred A. Knopf.

Martin, P. S. 1963. *The Last 10,000 Years: A Fossil Pollen Record of the American Southwest.* Tucson: University of Arizona Press.

Martin, W. C., and C. R. Hutchins. 1980. *A Flora of New Mexico.* Vol. 1, publ. D-3300. Braunschweig, West Germany: J. Cramer.

Maxwell, R. A. 1985. *Big Bend Country: A History of Big Bend National Park.* Big Bend National Park: Big Bend Natural History Association.

Morafka, J. D. 1977. *A Biogeographical Analysis of the Chihuahuan Desert.* The Hague: W. Junk.

Murphy, D. 1984. *The Guadalupes.* Carlsbad, N.M.: Carlsbad Caverns–Guadalupe Mountains Association.

Northington, D. K., and T. L. Burgess. 1979. "Status of Rare and Endangered Plant Species of the Guadalupe Mountains National Park, Texas." In Genoways and Baker, *Biological Investigations in the Guadalupe Mountains National Park, Texas*. National Park Service Proceedings and Transactions Series no. 4. Washington, D.C.: U.S. Government Printing Office.

————. 1979. "Summary of the Vegetative Life Zones of the Guadalupe Mountains National Park, Texas." In Genoways and Baker, *Biological Investigations in the Guadalupe Mountains National Park, Texas*. National Park Service Proceedings and Transactions Series no. 4. Washington, D.C.: U.S. Government Printing Office.

Powell, A. M. 1988. *Trees and Shrubs of Trans-Pecos Texas*. Big Bend National Park: Big Bend Natural History Association.

————. 1994. *Grasses of the Trans-Pecos and Adjacent Areas*. Austin: University of Texas Press.

Raisz, E. 1959. *Landforms of Mexico*. Map prepared for the Geography Branch of the Office of Naval Research, Cambridge, Massachusetts.

Schneider-Hector, D. 1993. *White Sands: The History of a National Monument*. Albuquerque: University of New Mexico Press.

Spaulding, W. G., and P. S. Martin. 1979. "Ground Sloth Dung of the Guadalupe Mountains." In Genoways and Baker, *Biological Investigations in the Guadalupe Mountains National Park, Texas*. National Park Service Proceedings and Transactions Series no. 4. Washington, D.C.: U.S. Government Printing Office.

Warnock, B. H. 1970. *Wildflowers of the Big Bend Country, Texas*. Alpine, Tex.: Sul Ross State University.

————. 1974. *Wildflowers of the Guadalupe Mountains and the Sand Dune Country, Texas*. Alpine, Tex.: Sul Ross State University.

————. 1977. *Wildflowers of the Davis Mountains and Marathon Basin, Texas*. Alpine, Tex.: Sul Ross State University.

Wauer, R. 1971. "Ecological Distribution of Birds of the Chisos Mountains, Texas." *Southwest Naturalist* 16:1-29.

Weniger, D. 1991. *Cacti of Texas and Neighboring States: A Field Guide*. Austin: University of Texas Press.

INDEX OF FAMILY NAMES

*I*NDEX OF PLANT NAMES

About the Author

A biology teacher, naturalist, and enviromental activist, Steve West has extensive knowledge of the flora and fauna of the Chihuahuan Desert.

Carlsbad Caverns–Guadalupe Mountains Association

Founded in 1957, the Carlsbad Caverns-Guadalupe Mountains Association (CCGMA) is a private, nonprofit organization whose main objectives are to provide interpretation for the park visitor and to support the purposes and mission of the National Park Service at Carlsbad Caverns National Park, Guadalupe Mountains National Park, and the lands related to them in New Mexico and Texas. The goals of CCGMA are accomplished through educational programs utilizing a variety of media and scientific investigations resulting in a greater appreciation of those resources being conserved.

CCGMA operates bookshops at both national parks and at the National Park Administration Visitor Center in Carlsbad. Since 1957 CCGMA has donated more than two million dollars in support of the educational programs at Carlsbad Caverns and Guadalupe Mountains National Parks.

For more information on CCGMA, including information on membership and other publications, call (505) 785-2232 ext. 480, or visit www.ccgma.org.